The Teaching of English

LANGUAGE AND LANGUAGE LEARNING

Language and Language Learning

GENERAL EDITORS: R. MACKIN and P. D. STREVENS

The Teaching of English

Papers by

RANDOLPH QUIRK

JEREMY WARBURG

J. L. M. TRIM

W. H. MITTINS

B. C. BROOKES

J. C. CATFORD

Edited and introduced by

RANDOLPH QUIRK

A. H. SMITH

LONDON · *OXFORD UNIVERSITY PRESS* · 1964

Oxford University Press, Amen House, London EC4

GLASGOW NEW YORK TORONTO MELBOURNE WELLINGTON
BOMBAY CALCUTTA MADRAS KARACHI LAHORE DACCA
CAPE TOWN SALISBURY NAIROBI IBADAN ACCRA
KUALA LUMPUR HONG KONG

First published by Martin Secker and Warburg Ltd, 1959
First issued in Language and Language Learning, *1964*

© *Martin Secker and Warburg Ltd, 1959*

Printed in Great Britain by
Richard Clay and Company, Ltd, Bungay, Suffolk

Contents

Contributors

B. C. Brookes, M.A., Senior Lecturer in the Presentation of Technical Information in the Department of Electrical Engineering at University College London.

J. C. Catford, B.A., Director of the School of Applied Linguistics in the University of Edinburgh, now Professor of Linguistics and Director of the English Language Institute, University of Michigan.

W. H. Mittins, B.A., Lecturer in the Department of Education, University of Newcastle.

Randolph Quirk, M.A., Ph.D., Professor of English Language in the University of London.

A. H. Smith, O.B.E., Ph.D., D.Lit., F.S.A., Quain Professor of English in the University of London.

J. L. M. Trim, B.A., Lecturer in Phonetics in the University of Cambridge.

Jeremy Warburg, M.A., A.M., formerly Lecturer in English at University College London.

Preface

Since the latter part of 1957—by which time the papers in this volume had assumed their present form—the study of linguistics in all its aspects and applications has felt the exhilarating impact of the revaluations and excursions associated with the name of Noam A. Chomsky. The decision to re-issue the volume has raised interesting questions as to the kind and degree of revision that might appropriately reflect developments in these intervening years. After all, one of the books commended more than once below for its application of linguistics to English teaching, *Patterns of English* by Paul Roberts, has been explicitly superseded by *English Sentences*, in which the author re-presents his materials with a transformative-generative orientation. Moreover, within Great Britain too, there has been considerable work in linguistic studies and their application to the teaching of English, with the consequent appearance of practical text-books at various levels which go some way to reducing the force of long-standing complaints that teachers in schools, training colleges and universities have little opportunity of reforming their English language teaching. One thinks, for instance, of *A Grammar of Modern English* attractively presented for schools by one of our contributors, Mr W. H. Mittins, or of Professor Barbara Strang's more advanced and thoroughly stimulating *Modern English Structure*.

It is inevitable, then, that few of our contributors would present their papers in the precise form that seemed right in 1957. On the other hand, the argument for re-issuing the papers with only minor corrections of print and matters of fact has in the end been thought compelling. More hopeful and promising

PREFACE

the situation today may be, but the needs expressed in 1957 are no less great and no less urgent; our means of re-educating ourselves for the tasks of teaching English are rather richer, but the amount of re-education necessary has been little reduced, and in many ways the stumbling blocks to progress remain stubbornly as obtrusive.

We are grateful to Miss Joan Mulholland for her valuable help in preparing this edition.

RQ
AHS

May 1964

CHAPTER 1

Introduction
Randolph Quirk and A. H. Smith

The essays collected in this volume were delivered as a course of public lectures in the Communication Research Centre at University College London, in the spring of 1958. They deal with a problem which is very much in the public mind today, and one which is likely to remain so; for the use of the English language as a means of communication between individuals, and between sections of the community, and, indeed, between nations is of the greatest importance in considering the field of human relations. The ability to use English efficiently is—it can scarcely be repeated too often—an asset in every walk of life. Industrialists, scientists, and technologists are becoming increasingly aware of the value of this asset.

The teaching of English is obviously of comparable importance, and the essays here presented will stimulate a review of our present position. They are concerned with points which have emerged in the study of our written language, of English speech, and of linguistics generally; not least, they emphasize the special problems that are involved in the discriminating use of English in a social context.

Compared with the antiquity of English language and literature, the *teaching* of English is a very recent phenomenon, with which we have not, even yet, completely come to terms. In 1906, a Board of Education report drew attention to the confusion of aims in English teaching: apparently, the only well-established feature was the outcry of complaint—about the quality of the teaching, the unsuitable text-books, and the lack of any coherent sense of purpose. It is a depressing fact that, in its general terms, this report—like the others that have followed it—still has a topical ring; it has never 'dated', as it surely ought to have done. Since 1906, text-books, 'methods', and even books called 'The Teaching of English' have multiplied with remarkable fertility. The magnificent report of the Board of Education in 1921 (*The Teaching of English in England*) examined clearly and at length the problems which beset the teachers of English; this document was, and indeed still is, of fundamental importance, and it should be far more widely known today. Scholar has followed scholar in attempting to analyse what is wrong, but the problems remain; in fact—notably in language teaching—they have become more acute.

It has been customary to devote much time to the idea of teaching 'correct' English, but it has always been difficult to define what is meant by 'correct' English. Usually it is regarded as the application of the rules of Latin grammar and syntax to the English language, a notion which is, of course, fundamentally unsound. Sometimes it refers to the use of 'Received Standard English Pronunciation', sometimes to the cultivation of a 'literary' style—though the latter is almost always inappropriate in speech. In fact, the circumstances of utterance are extremely diverse, and one of the more realistic criteria of 'correctness' is that the linguistic forms selected should communicate the intended 'content' without unintentional obtrusion of 'expression'.

Protests against the most obvious excesses of the older kinds of language teaching have been heeded far more readily than appeals to reach agreement on what to substitute for them. As long ago as 1931, J. H. Fowler was writing: 'The outcry of a few years ago against the study of grammar in elementary schools, however reasonable as a protest against the shibboleths of grammatical labels and the wearisome and mechanical practice of parsing and elaborate tabular analyses, had some lamentable results. Sometimes one is tempted to think that the grammatical incoherency of the popular press at the present day may be accounted for by that period of English educational history in which grammar was recklessly abandoned' (*The Art of Teaching English*, p. 141). Yet, three years later, P. B. Ballard published his widely acclaimed book on *Teaching the Mother Tongue*, in which eight of the thirteen chapters bear the title 'The Limitations of Grammar', and in which the eighth ends without greater enthusiasm than to state that, although his 'attitude towards the teaching of grammar is sceptical' (as no one would doubt having read so far in his book), he regards 'the question as one to be looked into'.

It has, of course, been 'looked into' from time to time since then. One need mention only a few of the relevant publications: I. A. Gordon, *The Teaching of English* (London, 1947), especially chapter 5; *The Teaching of English in Schools*, edited by V. de Sola Pinto (London, 1950), especially Dr Pamela Gradon's interesting essay on 'The Teaching of Grammar'; and, perhaps most useful of all, the two chapters on 'The Need for a Linguistic Discipline' and 'English Language' in *English in Education*, by H. Blamires (London, 1951). But little effect has been felt,[1] and J. H. Fowler's words quoted above could well have been written in 1958. Many, very like them, were in fact written in 1958.

We have seen in the last half-dozen years a striking revival of interest in the English language and in the teaching of it at many levels, for many purposes, and to many nations. Among the English-speaking peoples, there has been widespread dissatisfaction at the decline of English language teaching in schools, training colleges, and universities. A British newspaper gave typical expression to this in a recent leading article which ended with the words: 'The art of grammar was, after all, the traditional occupation of the grammar schools. Let them look to it.' Many have deplored the ambiguity and turgidity that is prevalent in

---

[1] Five years after Blamires, the *Memorandum on the Teaching of English* issued by the Association of Assistant Mistresses in Secondary Schools (London, 1956) seems to be uninfluenced by recent movements and suggestions. The corresponding male association, the I.A.A.M., appears to have been only a little more receptive; see *The Teaching of English*, 2nd edn (Cambridge, 1957).

scientific, official, and legal writings; there have been demands (with what justification need not for the moment concern us) that the utterances of civil servants, scientists, technologists, and others dealing with matters of crucial public importance must be made comprehensible and clear. The Hill Report of Her Majesty's Government in July 1957 expressed the urgency of increasing and improving the teaching of English as a foreign language. As Professor Bruce Pattison has said, 'English is assuming a range of functions no other language has ever exercised before . . . and to see that the innumerable kinds and degrees of ability to use the language are attainable by those who need them is a tremendous educational problem and perhaps also a social and political one.'[1] 'There is, moreover,' wrote Dr E. M. W. Tillyard and others, in *The Times*, 3 February 1959, 'good reason to believe that more systematic study of general linguistics, with special reference to modern English, would benefit greatly not only the teaching of foreigners but the education of our own children, about whose command of their native tongue many complaints are made, not least by scientists', and in urging that funds should be speedily made available for the pursuit of this work, they express grave dissatisfaction with our present backwardness: 'Nowhere in our educational system is there adequate provision for research and training in the methods of teaching modern English, either to foreigners or to our own children.' Teaching English has assumed, almost suddenly, a new and dramatic importance.

The papers here collected reflect this great new interest in the English language and the widespread need that is being felt for new directions in its teaching. They seek to discuss our present-day problems with the language as they are encountered in the education of children and of adults, of native speakers and of foreigners; they seek to examine the theories underlying and the aims informing the teaching of English; they explore means of applying these theories and of realizing these aims. Above all, they seek to discuss the teaching of English in the light of the

[1] *English Teaching in the World Today* (London, 1950), pp. 2 f.

now considerable amount of research that has been accomplished or begun in the field of language study.

We are, of course, aware that we are far from covering the entire and complex subject of English teaching. For one thing, there is somewhat less emphasis on *how* to teach than on *what* to teach and *why* it is important to teach it. Moreover, we have narrowed our field still more by concentrating on one aspect—the teaching of English Language—where the need is recognized as most acute. Even in this restricted area, we are not so sanguine as to believe that this small volume offers large-scale or permanent solutions to problems that have beset the teaching profession for more than half a century. But we feel that we have made some contribution in calling attention to the results that have been achieved, particularly in linguistic scholarship, by the successors of Whitney and Sweet. The lines that such scholarship has been following are indicated in the chapters which follow: here it may be relevant to mention in addition that a start has been made on surveying present-day educated English usage in its many forms, with a view ultimately to the preparation of realistic and practical teaching-grammars.

CHAPTER 2

English Language and the Structural Approach | *Randolph Quirk*

I

With the changes of method in education and in linguistic analysis itself during the twentieth century, it is not perhaps surprising that opinion should have varied sharply throughout this period on the methods, the kind, the amount, and even the usefulness of English Language teaching in the educational establishments of the English-speaking countries.

Not that the nineteenth-century situation at its best has lacked staunch defenders on any of these counts. In his autobiography, Sir Winston Churchill tells us that, through being taught the old and rigorous English grammar, he 'gained an immense advantage over the cleverest boys. They all went on to learn Latin and Greek and splendid things like that. But I was taught English. We were considered such dunces that we could learn only English. Mr Somervell—a most delightful man, to whom my debt is great—was charged with the duty of teaching the stupidest boys the most disregarded thing—namely, to write mere English. He knew how to do it. . . . Not only did we learn English parsing thoroughly, but we also practised continually English analysis. Mr Somervell had a system of his own. He took a fairly long sentence and broke it up into its components by means of black, red, blue, and green inks. Subject, verb, object: Relative Clauses, Conditional Clauses, Conjunctive, and Disjunctive Clauses! Each had its colour and its bracket. It was a kind of drill. We did it almost daily. . . . Thus I got into my bones the essential structure of the ordinary British sentence—which is a noble thing. And when in after years my schoolfellows who had won prizes and distinction for writing such beautiful Latin poetry and pithy Greek epigrams had to come down to common English, to earn their living or make their way, I did not feel myself at any disadvantage. Naturally I am biased in favour of boys learning English. I would make them all learn English: and then let the clever ones learn Latin as an honour, and Greek as a treat. But the only thing I would whip them for is not knowing English. I would whip them for that.'[1]

No doubt, Sir Winston is making points here to which few educators (or linguists) would now wholeheartedly subscribe. Yet many would prefer the solidity of Mr Somervell's 'system of his own' to no grammar teaching at all, and after some decades in which English Language has been the neglected, almost moribund, poor relation in our syllabuses, there are clear signs that educators would like to re-instate the subject if only the linguists would tell them how.[2] And certainly, the lay public, never perhaps entirely happy about the decline in grammar teaching, have grown increasingly restive about the state of English linguistic knowledge and skill possessed by the younger generation. Indeed, one of the most remarkable educational phenomena of the past few years is the extent to which English Language has become a talking point: broadcasts and newspaper articles have reflected the keen and increased interest in the structure and variety of English expression and have given voice to the considerable disquiet that is felt over the degree of ignorance and naivety on linguistic matters; they have raised again and again questions about the extent and function of English Language teaching in our schools, training colleges, and universities.[3]

[1] *My Early Life* (London, 1930), pp. 30–1.

[2] Cf. F. Whitehead in *The Journal of Education*, vol. 88 (1956), pp. 454–6, and vol. 89 (1957), pp. 192–7.

[3] For instance, *Times Educational Supplement*, 11 September 1955; *The Listener*, 30 August 1956; *Daily Telegraph*, 31 August and 7 September 1957; *The Times*, 2 January 1958 (p. 3 and leading article).

All this has come about through the converging of a number of independent lines of thinking and development which it is not my present purpose to explore. Rather, it has been my privilege to write the first of the papers in this symposium, which is a reflex of the new interest in the English language and of the widespread need that is being expressed for better English teaching. In the present essay, the concern is going to be primarily with English Language teaching at home, to native English speakers, in the light, not specifically of new work so much as of work which ought to be known well beyond the specialized circle of linguists and philologists.

II

Now traditionally, English Language has been taught along with English Literature, and although voices have been raised against it, I think this is most certainly the right procedure. A good part of the purpose of teaching English Language is—or ought to be— to sharpen awareness of the medium, to make pupils understand and react fully to the medium at its subtlest, and thereby to encourage them to exploit the language's potentialities in their own use of it. This can best be done, as has long seemed natural, by bringing to the attention of our pupils, as material for such study, our noblest literature, produced by the pens of those who have, by common consent, been able to make best use of the language. This is not—be it noticed—making language study the handmaiden of literary studies (though I see good reason why it should be proud so to serve *as well*): rather, I am saying the opposite—that in the study of language, literature should be there as a handmaiden, just as I believe that literature is best studied when the study of language is to hand as an ancillary. Language study and teaching have an existence and value in their own right ('Man is the speaking animal. That is the main reason for studying speech'[1]), but the point I wish to make is that even from the most utilitarian viewpoint, the teaching of language needs literature among its prime material.

[1] James Sledd in *Language*, vol. 34 (1958), p. 139.

But such a happy, complementary relation does not appear to be widely recognized at present. In many schools and training colleges, language work of the old kind has declined and has not been replaced: indeed, there is (or has been till recently) some feeling that there is nothing to replace it with. And with justification. One has nothing but sympathy for teachers over the past few decades who have heard linguists convincingly damn the 'old grammar' and offer nothing but general principles in its place—offer, that is, no codification of the 'new grammar' in any form which could enable the harrassed teacher to take it into the classroom.[1]

Even at the present time, no grammar-book has been produced for British schools that carries the sanction of the professional linguist, and in the United States things are only slightly more advanced. There, too, linguists 'have found it easy to show the absurdity of much that is now taught but until quite recently they had not provided the better text-books which are necessary to the success of their argument';[2] there, too, some of the 'new grammars' to receive loudest acclaim have comprised little beyond the traditional lore, superficially purged of grosser misstatement but fundamentally unchanged. A notable example is R. C. Pooley's *Teaching English Grammar* (New York, 1957) which makes lofty claims (such as that 'grammar is the doorway to better composition') that are bound to seem empty when the 'grammar' comes down to stating that *John likes candy* ends with a noun 'in the accusative or objective case'. But some recent

[1] It is rather sad now to read through the considerable amount of work published on the problem of grammar teaching in the early nineteen-twenties. There is much of interest—largely because the difficulties have persisted—in the Board of Education's Departmental Report on *The Teaching of English in England*, published in 1921, and in the views of Sonnenschein, McKerrow, Mawer, Jespersen, and others which this Report caused to appear in the publications of the English Association (for example, Pamphlet No. 56, of July 1923) and elsewhere. There is little cause to be proud of what has been done in subsequent years to tackle the fundamental problems that were so fully debated at this time.

[2] Sledd in *Language*, vol. 33 (1957), p. 261.

American text-books have been pioneering feats which deserve close study; one could wish, for instance, that British teachers had available something comparable in modernity and comprehensiveness to the *Patterns of English* by Paul Roberts (New York, 1956) or—at a more sophisticated level—A. A. Hill's *Introduction to Linguistic Structures: From Sound to Sentence in English* (New York, 1958). It is certainly to be hoped that the American example of producing even imperfect incorporations of modern linguistic thought will not be as slow to be followed as was the case with the 'sentence method' of reading, an American manual on which appeared in 1881 though the method was not seriously used in this country until the nineteen-twenties.[1]

Our present position, then, as regards English Language teaching is virtually that our teachers live in a no man's land between the discredited old grammar and the unwritten new. And as teachers who have had no language training have been fed back into the schools, the law of diminishing returns has operated vigorously, prompting in the past year or so on the one hand a spate of angry letters in the press[2] complaining of the ignorance, linguistic naivety, and illiteracy itself obtrusive among the young, and on the other hand some tentative moves from literary critics towards exploring language structure and operation in a way serviceable to the study of literature, because so little work of this kind was being initiated by the 'language specialists'.[3]

From both these points of view, the clear need arises to re-invigorate or re-introduce English Language teaching in the schools and training colleges—and I repeatedly mention the training colleges because, obviously, unless the teacher in training becomes enthusiastic and competent, the great mass of children

[1] See the Ministry of Education Pamphlet No. 26, *Language* (London, 1954), p. 56.

[2] As in the *Daily Telegraph*, 3–14 September 1957.

[3] In the case of I. A. Richards, the moves have been rather more than tentative. See also my references to the work of H. Straumann and others, *Year's Work in English Studies*, vol. 36 (1955), pp. 38–9, and (in connexion with the criticism of earlier writings) J. Butt in the *Durham University Journal*, vol. 43 (1951), pp. 96–102.

can in no way get access to refreshed language teaching.[1] We need utilitarian English Language to defeat what has been called the new illiteracy and to cultivate linguistic ability, understanding, and urbane tolerance. Our present deficiencies in these matters are admirably demonstrated in the arguments and illustrations offered by Mr Mittins in Chapter 4. And although we may agree with Sweet that grammar is not very helpful to the native in his acquisition of communicative essentials,[2] nor 'of much use in correcting vulgarisms, provincialisms, and other linguistic defects, for these are more dependent on social influence at home and at school than on grammatical training', we cannot agree with those who think they thus have Sweet's authority for dismissing grammatical study from the curriculum. A grammatical training is invaluable for learning to see the 'vulgarisms' and 'provincialisms' objectively and in perspective, to see that while the line between standard and non-standard is often clear, its definition is rather arbitrary than based on inherent beauty and order versus ugliness and chaos. It helps, for example, to be shown the frequent use of preterite for past participle (*we/we have ~ ate/shook/broke/wrote*) in the light of the many verbs which ignore such a distinction in standard English (*we/we have ~ found/clung/dug/sat*), the inconsistency between *got* and *forgotten*, the British and American difference over *got(ten)*, and similar points.

It is a disheartening fact that we still find in educated professional people—teachers, journalists, public figures—the most alarming and preposterous naivety over matters like standard language and 'good' grammar. It was by no means an 'uneducated' man who sent Charles Morgan a post-card reading:

---

[1] Cf. H. Blamires, *English in Education* (London, 1951), p. 110: Teachers 'are giving poor instruction in English Language because they are not themselves sufficiently educated in respect of the meaning and use of words. We need a concentrated campaign to improve the teacher's own understanding of thought and language.'

[2] *New English Grammar* (Oxford, 1891), pt. 1, p. 5. The same point is illustrated with a racy New Zealand flavour by Professor I. A. Gordon: 'I speak English, don't I? My cobbers understand me. Why the heck should you have to teach me English at all?' *The Teaching of English* (London, 1947), p. 42.

'You who are supposed to be a master of language, what possible authority or excuse can you have for the disgusting American journalese of spelling the word *judgment* with an "e"?' Morgan was able to reply, 'My authority for what you call American journalese is the Book of Common Prayer',[1] but of course he did not need such devastating ammunition to shatter the miserable complaint of his correspondent, appalling in its ignorance and bigotry alike.

And from the other, the literary viewpoint too, if we are to have pupils explore the patterned sounds in a poem, strange powerful word-formations, deliberate collocations and tricks of word-order, we must teach them to explore their own language in linguistic terms. Proust saw the need for grammatical analysis to this end; in 1920 he wrote of Flaubert: 'Un homme qui par l'usage entièrement nouveau qu'il a fait du passé indéfini, du participe présent, de certains pronoms et de certaines préposi-tions, a renouvelé presque autant notre vision des choses que Kant avec ses Catégories, les théories de la Connaissance et de la Réalité du monde extérieur', and as Professor Ullmann says, on quoting this, one might be excused for imagining the writer to be a linguist who exaggerated the importance of grammar.[2] But Proust is not an isolated example. W. H. Gardner found that a comparable grasp of linguistic description was necessary for examining the work of Gerard Manley Hopkins, and more recently it has become increasingly common for literary critics to see the need for a study of language in linguistic terms.

III

'Language in linguistic terms' sounds tautologous, but in fact it is crucial.[3] It was largely language in non-linguistic terms that

[1] *On Learning to Write* (English Association Presidential Address, Oxford, 1954), pp. 3 f.

[2] *Style in the French Novel* (Cambridge, 1957), p. 94.

[3] It is worth noting that Professor W. S. Allen entitled his recent inaugural lecture in the Cambridge Chair of Comparative Philology *On the Linguistic Study of Languages* (Cambridge, 1957).

brought much of the older teaching to a confused end in the twenties: language in non-linguistic terms far more, I think, than English in Latin terms. And this is the more to be regretted in that a good deal of the older teaching did not deserve to end in chaos and did so only because it was associated with much that was justly discredited, so that thereafter it was not easy to distinguish the damned from the innocent. When I was at school in the twenties, the old grammar was still taught in all its rigour, and I have never been inclined to regret it. But much of it was indeed unhelpful, chiefly—it seems to me now—because it was language in non-linguistic terms. A noun, I learnt, was the name of a person, place, or thing: but the name of a thing, like *ship*, always seemed in some irritatingly indefinable way to be grammatically different from the name of a person or place, like *Billie* and *England*; almost any sentence, such as *The ship was called Venus*, drew attention to the fact that the two nouns were not precisely analogous, that there was something wrong with our definition. Moreover, *red* is the name of a colour, which is a thing, and *mollify* is the name of an action, but teacher would not agree that these were nouns. No, he would say, the name of an action is another part of speech—the verb, and that is where *mollify* belongs. And yet words like *taxation* which seemed so obviously names of actions were not verbs but nouns.

Similar difficulties occurred with other terms like 'subject' and 'object'. Nesfield had it that the Direct Object was the thing towards which the action of the verb was directed, while the Indirect Object was the person for whom the action was done; these distinctions seemed quite unrelated to the facts of language when one considered examples like *Bill gave Harry the money*, *Harry was given the money by Bill*, and *The money was given to Harry by Bill*, since the definitions made *money* the Direct Object and *Harry* the Indirect Object in each case.[1]

---

[1] Definitions which ignore parallels and contrasts in linguistic structure continue to appear. According to Miss A. G. Hatcher, *bad weather* is subject and object respectively in *bad weather was likely* and *bad weather was forecast*; see *Word*, vol. 12 (1956), especially pp. 239 ff.

But this does not mean that the terms 'noun' and 'verb', 'subject' and 'object' have no relevance for English. It is not the adaptation of Latin terms to English grammar that lets us down. This is not, of course, to deny the well-established principle that it is undesirable and even dangerous to describe one language in terms evolved for another; such a procedure can lead to the creation of wholly artificial categories which are worse than value-less—as when missionaries sought to reduce Chinese to the terms of Latin structure. But English is an Indo-European language as Latin is, and in practice we find that very many of the terms which are useful for describing Latin are useful for English too, and since the languages studied by English-speaking people are always Indo-European ones (if any), it is a pedagogical virtue to have as nearly as possible a single terminology for all of them. No, the trouble is not that the Latin terms do not suit English, it is that the non-linguistic frame of reference does not suit language. The old definitions do not satisfactorily distinguish *ship* and *red* and *mollify* and *taxation*, subject and object, but English does indeed distinguish all these and they are valuable cate-gories. A structural approach seeks to show their validity in terms of language itself and demonstrates how essential these categories are to the operation of our signalling system.

The notion of 'system' is important to this approach and a language has been defined as a *structured system of arbitrary sounds and sound-sequences which is used in communication and which is a fairly complete catalogue of the things, events, and processes in a given environment.*[1] Language is a structured system—language is systematic and patterned: English adverbs characteristically end in *-ly*; nouns form plurals with [s], [z], or [iz] according to the econo-mically statable nature of the stem ending; subject systematically precedes verb and verb precedes object, so that an utterance like *Jones killed Brown* is unambiguous. Now, it is at the phonological level that linguistic structure has best been demonstrated in the post-Saussurean period, so we might glance for a moment at this well-known material and see some of its implications for study at

[1] Cf. J. B. Carroll, *The Study of Language* (Cambridge, Mass., 1953), p. 10.

other levels. But first let me make the point that not *all* human vocal noises are structured and systematic to the same extent or in the same way; we must place on a separate footing the grunts, giggles, and sounds of annoyance that are relatively our personal contribution to speech. Thus, when one says '[æx] I've dropped my pen', [æx] is not part of English structure in the same way as *I've dropped my pen* is; another speaker, or the same speaker on a different day, might say '[u:] (or [ou]) I've dropped my pen', without a witness being able to say that the utterances were different. The exclamation may be given dozens of phonetic realizations, or none at all, but there is much less variation tolerable with *I've dropped my pen*; here we have a closely interdependent structure which permits no such extreme variant as [u:v dript mou paun].

Not that all grammarians realize on how different a footing exclamations stand from other elements in a language—how ephemeral and individual they may be, for instance. Many examples of failure to distinguish between structured and nonstructured, current and obsolete, graphic and phonic can be found in the long chapter on exclamations in a comprehensive grammar of English published in Paris in 1949.[1] 'Si *My God!* peut échapper à un homme, une femme dira seulement *My!*' '*Flac! Flac!* imite un bruit clapotant.' '*Sa sa sa!* figure une marche militaire.' '*Tik tak!* imite la pendule.' 'On pleure: *Uh, uh!*' 'Le coq fait *cock-a-doodle-doo*; la poule, *cock-cock*.' To order a horse leftwards the English is *hait-wo*, to the right, *gee, gee-ho, ree*. 'Pour arrêter un cheval, [on dit] *joss! stank!*' 'Pour guider une vache, [on dit] *prou!*' 'Pour s'adresser aux porcs, *tig!*' The drollness of some of these examples lies partly in their failure to correspond with such facts as one knows of these matters, but partly also in that few grammarians consider that their task embraces teaching pupils to address themselves to pigs and the like. Yet even in less bucolic contexts, the exclamations in this grammar are scarcely less bizarre. Disgust is said to be expressed by *fie, fudge, harrow*, and *whew*; impatience by *buzz, whip*, and *pop*; joy by *he, hey-day*,

[1] C. Cestre and M.-M. Dubois, *Grammaire complète de la langue anglaise.*

indeed, and *aha*; sorrow by *alack*, *alas*, *heigho*, *well-away*, and *just my luck*.[1] These illustrate several infelicities in the art and science of grammar-writing, but my point with them here is to emphasize the need to distinguish strata of loosely structured noises from the bed-rock of tightly structured ones in a language. There is much useful work to be done on the system underlying exclamatory noises, as Mr Catford reminds us below,[2] but no progress will be made if one does not recognize that they operate on a distinct plane of their own, with their own limits of tolerance.

In the view of most linguists, the bed-rock just referred to consists of the phonemic system. It has been found that out of the thousands of different human sounds isolated and described by phoneticians, no language uses more than three dozen or so as contrastive sounds which distinguish words. Polish uses a 'dark *l*' in contrast with a 'clear *l*'; English speakers use similar varieties of *l* (often, in *doll* and *leap* respectively), but not in contrast: to us they seem the 'same' sound because the difference is not deliberate but depends on the phonetic context. Welsh has a voiceless *l* in contrast with a voiced one, and although we sometimes use a similar voiceless *l* (often, in *play*), it again depends wholly on the phonetic context and if we try to make the sound in a different position, it seems difficult (as in *Llandudno*). On the other hand, we distinguish *k* and *g* as two quite different sounds, whereas the Tamil speakers of India find the English distinction and distribution of the sounds difficult since they are treated as one in Tamil. It is almost always the case with another language's small group of phonemes that we find some of them hard: this is not a matter of inherent difficulty but only of unfamiliarity—they do not belong to our system and clash with the long acquired habits of our speech organs. So when we borrow a word from a foreign language, we tend to anglicize it by substituting English sounds which seem to us nearest to the foreign ones. However *Jerez* was pronounced when we adopted the name, we can be

[1] See further *Modern Language Review*, vol. 46 (1951), pp. 74 f.

[2] P. 149, Cf. also D. Abercrombie's plea for the study of gesture, *English Language Teaching*, vol. 9 (1954), pp. 3–12.

confident that it was not as 'English' as *sherry*. So too in other languages. *Screwdriver* seems a perfectly easy word to us, but in languages whose speakers do not pronounce more than one consonant at a time without a vowel between, the cluster [skr] seems impossibly difficult; in the Hausa language of Nigeria and the Sudan, in fact, the word has been adopted as *sukurudireba*.

Thus new adoptions and new coinages normally conform to patterns already existing—and this has important analogies at all linguistic levels. Phonologically, it means that new words in English have to employ sounds from the repertoire of some forty phonemes of which are constructed our existing half-million words. And not only that. One is not permitted unrestricted permutations of these forty sounds: otherwise, we could introduce [ʒaud] or [ŋɔšk] as new words, since they embody only English sounds. Yet such forms seem utterly foreign because the distribution of the sounds is also restricted in the system: [ʒ] and [ŋ] are English sounds but they do not occur initially, and [š] does not occur before [k]. We have just noticed that English permits more consonant clustering than some languages (compare *screw, stripped, bridge, flummoxed, triumphs*), yet these conform to restrictive patterns, the rules for which can be set down on half a sheet of paper. These rules will show that the detergent manufacturers will not loose upon English-speaking markets monosyllabic names like [škwipf] or [gnɔiðb] or [ʒdæf].

All this is by no means to endorse Meillet's triumphant 'chaque langue forme un système où tout se tient'. Few scholars today are optimistic about uncovering a single system which will embrace all the facets of a language: it is more likely that a language is a complex of interlocking, even overlapping systems, as we proceed from one sort of usage to another (from familiar slangy exchanges, for example, to elevated learned discourse) or as we proceed from one level of analysis to another (for example, from sounds to syntax). But that language is systemic, is structured, few would now deny.

IV

So language functions by systematically ignoring a whole host of phonetic differences which speakers choose to regard as trivial (for example, in English, the difference between the *l*-sounds of *play*, *doll*, *leap*), and by concentrating on a small number of distinctions marking the thirty or forty phonemes. But this is by no means the whole phonological story. We do not have to hear or utter every phoneme equally distinctly when linguistic exchanges take place.

If one sees a woman with a pail sitting on a stool milking a large animal in the half dark, one does not have to see its horns or hear it moo before deciding whether the animal is a cow or a horse. In language, similarly, the context of situation, the context of a word, the context of a sound may often provide enough clues to comprehension without our needing to hear all the possible linguistic symbols. You take someone to a telephone and show him how to make his call: he may then say, without seeming to use indistinct or uneducated English, [ã: 'vɛi 'gei²f: jə 'hɛlp], though this ignores or replaces several of the 'essential' sounds of English, because the context of situation makes them unnecessary. Grammatical context can also provide such high determinacy that optimum discrimination of parts may be unnecessary: as with the construction *I have got to* (*go*). It is obvious that one must class *t*, *d*, *r* as significantly different sounds in English; they mark, after all, the difference between *tug*, *dug*, and *rug* or *toll*, *dole*, *and roll*. But the interdependence of the parts of *I have got to* can allow the neutralization of this *t-d-r* contrast so that one may hear *I have got to go*, *I've got to go*, *I've gotta go*, *I gotta go*, *I godda go*, *I gorra go*. We adopted the word *potage* from French and it is now *porridge*; in the context [pɔ-idʒ], the English phonemic contrast between *t*, *d*, and *r* was not required.

There are interesting analogies in printed and written English where we have twenty-six distinct letter shapes but do not always need to see all their distinctive parts with equal clarity for immediate comprehension. When we are learning to read, we are

like the foreigner who utters distinctly all the parts of *I have got to*:
we concentrate on each letter as a whole and in a linear fashion,
regarding each as unpredictable as the one before. Later, our

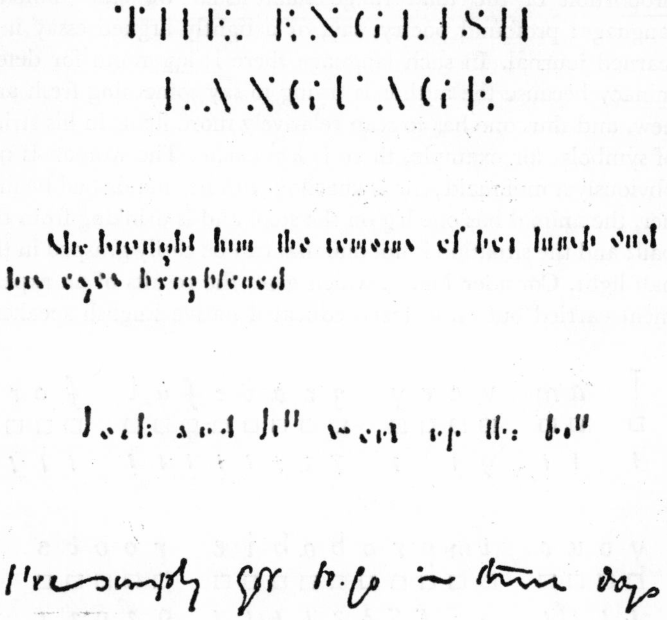

THE ENGLISH
LANGUAGE

She brought him the remains of her lunch and
his eyes brightened

Jack and Jill went up the hill

I'll be simply gr hlp in three days

FIG. 1

reading habits enable us to treat shapes and sequences of letters
much more cavalierly—and our handwriting often reflects this
only too well. Consider Fig. 1.[1]

With both oral and visual language, then, context and prob-

---

[1] A start has only recently been made on the close study of written language.
One may consult 'The Analysis of Written Middle English' by A. McIntosh
(who is preparing a monograph on 'graphemics') in the *Transactions of the
Philological Society* for 1956, and R. A. Crossland's 'Graphic Linguistics and its
Terminology' in the *Proceedings of the University of Durham Philosophical Society*
for 1957; in both these articles there are useful references to other writings in
this field.

ability encourage us to dispense with the discriminations at our disposal. But with some utterances and texts we cannot dispense with them so readily. Language which requires us to use a higher proportion of the total range than usual we call 'difficult' language: profound poetry, say, or a tightly argued essay in a learned journal. In such language there is less room for determinacy because the author is trying to say something fresh and new, and thus one has to scan relatively more items in his string of symbols; for example, there is less cliché. The woman is not obviously a milkmaid; she is kneeling with her hands tied behind her, the animal has one leg on the stool and is drinking from the pail: and the situation is not one that can be easily grasped in the half light. Consider Fig. 2, which gives the results of an experiment carried out on a dozen educated native English speakers.

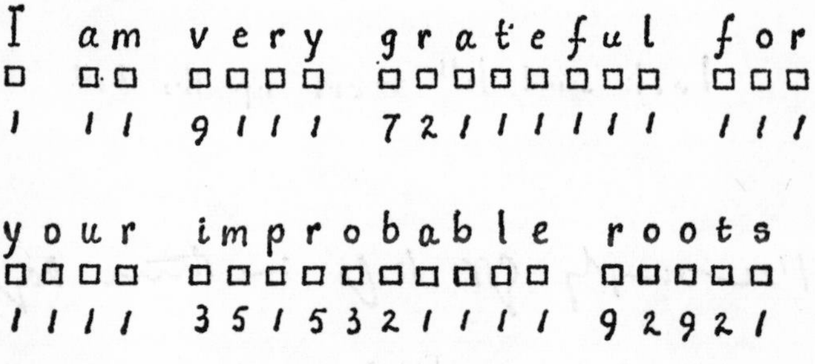

I am very grateful for
□ □·□ □□□□ □□□□□□□□ □□□
1 1 1 9 1 1 1 7 2 1 1 1 1 1 1 1 1 1

your improbable roots
□□□□ □□□□□□□□□□ □□□□□
1 1 1 1 3 5 1 5 3 2 1 1 1 1 9 2 9 2 1

Fig. 2

The sentence was set down as a series of smudges and spaces, each smudge corresponding to a letter, each space to a word boundary; the subjects were asked to guess each letter in turn and the figures are the average number of guesses required to achieve the right answer. Thus *I am* appeared to be virtually certain as the two words in that position and in that order; *very* gave no trouble once the *v* had been established, and *grateful* was achieved similarly. At this point, the results show how *for* is structurally determined, coming as readily as the *-ful* element of *grateful*. But the last two words gave a steady degree of trouble: individual symbols carried a heavier signalling load in direct proportion to their lack of contextual determinacy; the language had become 'difficult'. Yet one may note, even within the highly unexpected word *improbable*, the dependence of *p* on the preceding *m*, the predictability of the ending *-able* and of the plural *-s* of *roots*.

It is clear that the signalling load on symbols varies considerably throughout an utterance. In some cases, we need the full range of discriminations; at other points, predictability makes it possible to dispense with some of them, so that beneath the level of optimum discriminations, we may discern a coarser mesh of distinctions which function adequately on occasion. In phonology, several lines of inquiry within the past decade have led to the postulation of just such a coarser mesh—a series of what are called 'distinctive features'.[1] By this hypothesis, it is not a matter of distinguishing one phoneme from all the others that concerns us in the use of language, but rather of distinguishing one from a much smaller number of fundamental binary contrasts which do not usually total more than eight in any one language (for instance, what Jakobson, Fant, and Halle call 'vocalic/consonantal', 'compact/diffuse', 'grave/acute'). A given phoneme, when being used with maximum discrimination, is viewed as being a bundle of such distinctive features (thus *t* is, among other things, consonantal, diffuse, and acute), but when the phoneme is in contexts where maximum discrimination is not required, the number of distinctive features may be much reduced. Again, an analogy at the graphic level seems close and inviting. As Fig. 1 shows, the practised reader does not require all the characteristic distinguishing parts of a letter at all times; it seems likely that he finds it necessary only to notice 'distinctive features', such as ascenders and descenders, the breadth of an *m* and the slenderness of an *i*.

[1] See R. Jakobson, C. G. M. Fant and M. Halle, *Preliminaries to Speech Analysis* (Cambridge, Mass., 1952).

V

At the grammatical level, it is often easiest to reveal linguistic structure by avoiding ordinary English. Confronted with a series like this, *Croatations ungleshably polanians pleakful ruggle plome rit the the in*, one immediately acknowledges that, so far as English speakers can see, this is shapeless nonsense, completely un-English except for individual syllables. But rearranged like this,

Plome the pleakful croatations ruggle polanians ungleshably in the rit,

while it may remain somewhat mysterious, it has structure, and young people will speedily join in identifying the parts of speech and discussing their basis of identification. Nouns, verbs, adjectives, adverbs, and prepositions are shown to be such by reason of their position, form, inflexion, and contrast with each other. We are led away from the idea of words necessarily being in themselves 'parts of speech', and towards the idea of syntactic structures in which words operate as the movable parts.[1] One can distinguish between the kinds of adverb represented by *plome* and *ungleshably*, and one can discover another kind of adverb by placing *plome* immediately before *ungleshably*. Subject and object are distinguished on the basis of their respective grammatical functions, and the part played by word-order as a structural feature of English can be discussed. One can demonstrate the parts played by intonation and juncture in English by reading the utterance out in different forms, and asking the pupils what difference each change has introduced; they become alive, in consequence, to the factors which produce subtle nuances in their language.

All these things can of course be accomplished through the use of ordinary English: that is how all native speakers learnt the

[1] 'Since word-class status depends for its recognition on syntagmatic differences, it appears reasonable to make the latter the main object of description' (T. F. Mitchell, 'Syntagmatic Relations in Linguistic Analysis', *Transactions of the Philological Society*, 1958, p. 103).

structural features of the language and how we all came to know them intuitively. But once we have reached the stage when this knowledge is indeed intuitive, it is probably easier to induce an intellectual and conscious grasp of them through structured nonsense, with 'meaning' deliberately filtered off. It is in any case a salutary lesson, and often a surprise, to discover that grammar exists outside what is ordinarily called meaning, or rather that grammar is an important dimension of meaning: that it has a meaning of its own which is not so easily discerned when we are confronted with words which have a meaning in the dictionary sense. For example, given the words *man tiger ate*, pupils will decide which ate which purely from lexical meaning; given *blim ate blom*, they will decide the same issue on structural grounds alone; with *blim blom ate*, they would lack the clues both of lexical and grammatical meaning. Thus structural meaning is most easily demonstrated when lexical meaning is removed; the significance of word-order, inflexion, intonation is readily apparent when there is no other kind of significance to attract and deflect our conscious attention.[1]

In morphology, too, nonsense formations are useful in presenting—or indeed determining—how much we know from the forms of words and their affixes. We recognize *pleakful* in the sequence above as an adjective from its position and from its suffix *-ful*; and by reason of the *-ful* we can infer the noun *pleak*, because it is a feature of English morphology that many nouns yield corresponding adjectives on this pattern. Similarly, while the position and inflexion of *croatations* indicate that it is a noun, the suffix *-ation* helps us to classify it among nouns; we can introduce the subject of what an abstract noun is and discuss the relation between nouns in *-ation* and verbs in *-ate*—in this case, *croatate*. *Ruggle* is a verb with a preterite *ruggled*, and the discussion of why we do not think it a verb like *dig* with a preterite *dug* again

---

[1] Cf. C. C. Fries, *The Structure of English* (New York, 1952), pp. 70–2. A slightly different technique to the same end is suggested by J. R. Firth in *Studies in Linguistic Analysis* (Special Volume of the Philological Society, Oxford, 1957), p. 8.

helps one to grasp intellectually what was previously known only intuitively. We can even make suggestions about a kind of aspectual meaning with this verb by reason of the analogy of our frequentative series of English verbs like *sparkle*, *gabble*, *wriggle*. Polanians, even with a small *p*, are probably human beings, members of some association or brotherhood; perhaps they adhere to the creed of *polany* (which brings in the question of systematic variations of stress), or perhaps they practise, behind closed doors, the vice of polany. *Ungleshably* is the manner of doing something which cannot be *gleshed*.

In this way, we bring out the meaningful contrast in which our grammatical forms operate, and we show that they operate in a tightly ordered, harmonious system. We can show, too, that the disruption of this system produces incommunicable gibberish, as our first arrangement of the nonsense words above indicates; that our greatest literary artists have to communicate by means of this system; and that literature which is hard to understand (some of Dylan Thomas perhaps, and much of Joyce) is often difficult because it is compelling us to react to relatively rare patterns in the system, a kind of difficulty which it is important to distinguish from lexical difficulty or complexity of thought. Many of the curious and amusing forms in *Finnegans Wake*, for instance, require us to make morphemic associations in unfamiliar environments: *bashfully* conveying not only 'shamefacedly' but also, with a slangy twist, 'forcefully'; *omportent* embodying parts of 'omnipotent', 'important', and 'portentous'; *beehiviour* indicating the gregarious automatism of city life by the apian punning and the echo of Cockney pronunciation; *are you still tropeful of popetry*; *bespectable*, and many similar examples.[1] Part of the charm of Thomas's villanelle 'Do Not Go Gentle' is that the same word-group is used alternatively as an imperative and as an indicative.[2]

---

[1] Compare also Laforgue's formations like *sexciproque* and *sangsuelle*.

[2] More elaborate examples of syntactic patterning in English poetry are to be found in Donald Davie, *Articulate Energy* (London, 1955).

VI

The definition of language given earlier stated that it consisted of 'arbitrary sound-sequences', and this is directed against a naivety that is recurrent in every generation and which asserts that a rose by any other name does *not* smell as sweet. Words, as Locke said, 'come to excite in Men certain *Ideas*, so constantly and readily, that they are apt to suppose a natural connexion between them. But that they signify only Men's peculiar *Ideas*, and that *by a perfectly arbitrary imposition*, is evident, in that they often fail to excite in others (even that use the same Language) the same *Ideas*, we take them to be the Signs of: And every Man has so inviolable a Liberty, to make Words stand for what *Ideas* he pleases, that no one hath the Power to make others have the same *Ideas* in their minds, that he has, when they use the same Words, that he does.'[1]

An implicit belief in this 'natural connexion' is as widespread as ever. There seem to be countless thousands who believe, consciously or unconsciously, that the English show the genuineness of their love for dogs by calling them *dogs* rather than something absurdly uncharacteristic and inappropriate like *chiens* or *Hunde*. 'Look at them, sir,' says Aldous Huxley's old Rowley in *Crome Yellow*, pointing at a number of swine wallowing in the mud, 'rightly is they called pigs.' It ought to be part of everyone's education to be liberated from emotional naiveties about words, or at any rate to have the bases for emotional fads pointed out so that one has the chance of acquiring a relatively sophisticated and objective attitude to language.

Now, there is a real sense in which certain sound-sequences, partly by reason of the morphemic associations we have been discussing, lose part of their arbitrariness and become predominantly attached to certain senses. But this does not justify the common word-hysteria that produces violent letters in the

[1] *An Essay Concerning Humane Understanding* (1689), 4th edn (London, 1700), p. 237.

press calling (as recently) *transportation* 'a vile word', *layby* 'a dreadful . . . atrocity', *guts* and *job* 'most vulgar words'. In 1934, Dr Edward Lyttelton (in an English Association Pamphlet, be it noted) called the use of the adjective in 'This would be a tremendous guarantee of peace' an 'enormity', because *tremendous* (by the usual etymological argument) means 'that which makes us tremble'.[1] The story is told by Professor John Clark of an American professor who happened to mention to a girl student the fine litter of puppies just presented to him by his spaniel bitch, and he was distressed to find that he had reduced the girl to blushes. 'It's quite all right,' she blurted, for seeing his concern had added to her confusion. 'It's quite all right, only I'm not used to hearing that word applied to dogs.'

The sociological factor in the use of language must not be neglected. Some attempt must be made to see objectively the processes by which words become charged with emotion, get stigmatized as 'slangy', 'pompous', 'low', or even 'dirty'. The great forces of tabu of various kinds ought not to be ignored (as the words most affected have usually been by our lexicographers) if education is truly to increase our self-awareness: and I do mean tabu in its commonly accepted applications as well as the other important forms of it already exemplified. Pupils can but gain from an open discussion of why our dictionaries include some names (the learned ones) for bodily processes and omit the commoner, more universal ones—of why the boycott is aimed not at the designata, the referents themselves, but only at certain of the linguistic signs for them. For we must make no mistake: the fascination of these problems will make them occupy pupils' attention whether or not we give them informed guidance. It will be recalled how Dr Johnson was congratulated by well-meaning ladies for having omitted from his *Dictionary* what they called the 'naughty words', on which the Doctor's

---

[1] *The Claim of Our Mother Tongue* (Oxford, 1934), p. 5; there are several other examples of the misapplication of 'a little learning' to questions of English usage in this pamphlet, and of course still more in Fowler's *Modern English Usage* and similar books.

characteristic comment was, 'What, my dears, then you have been looking for them.'

It is easy and worthwhile to demonstrate that there is nothing inherently ugly or shocking about *guts* or *bitch* by inviting consideration of words like *shuts*, *cuts*, *bit*, *pitch*, *kitchen* which have similar features of phonological structure but which are not condemned as ugly or shocking; that these are no more inherently ugly than *pasture*, *languid*, and *breeze* are inherently beautiful. This is not to say that we may not have *private* views on the beauty or ugliness of words (Alice had no idea what latitude was, or longitude either, but she thought they were nice grand words to say): but we must become sufficiently socially adjusted in our linguistic reactions as not to be surprised if our personal tastes are not shared by others. It remains true that the English words which are directly motivated by their linguistic form in the direction of a particular meaning are few and far between (echoic and imitative words like *cuckoo* and *splash*), and that onomatopoeic effects often depend in fact partly on association of meaning as well as partly on the direct suggestion of natural sound-sequences: 'lake water lapping with low sounds by the shore'.

This problem has recently been explored by Mr John Press.[1] After quoting Valéry and F. E. Halliday, Press comments: 'Certain words are reputed to have an elemental significance incapsulated in their sound; a sequence of these words forms a cadence which, by means of onomatopoeia, melopoeia, and hypnotic rhythm, produces the required emotional effect in the reader.' As he says, this runs counter to the conclusions of men such as Burke (*On the Sublime and the Beautiful*) that 'words . . . have no sort of resemblance to the ideas for which they stand'; we have already noted Locke's views above. Press goes on:

---

[1] *The Fire and the Fountain* (Oxford, 1955), especially pp. 121–7. Other critics to expose the 'sound is sense' fallacy in recent years include I. A. Richards, *Practical Criticism* (London, 1929), especially pp. 231 ff; F. W. Bateson, *English Poetry: A Critical Introduction* (London, 1950), especially ch. I, 'The Primacy of Meaning'; W. K. Wimsatt, Jr., and M. C. Beardsley, *The Verbal Icon* (University of Kentucky Press, 1954), pp. 21 ff.

'When men complain of an ugly word, they are not, in fact, objecting to its sound. . . . The objection to such words as under-graduette and rodent operative is primarily a grammatical, intellectual, and moral objection, although we may sum up our dislike for the offensive phrases by saying that they sound hideous.' Those who speak of 'tonal values inherent in certain vowel-sounds' or who claim that Milton arranged sounds to resemble organ music ought to consider the extent to which such effects are produced by 'manipulation of associations'.[1]

A training in English language and criticism would thus help one to see that it is superficial, to say the least, to describe *guts*, the word, as ugly and vulgar. One ought to be helped to see that any offensiveness lies in the collocations of the word and in its associations (as with tough-looking women gutting herrings). The offensiveness is not in the form of the word, nor even in its lexical meaning; the metaphor of *guts* for *courage* is paralleled by a use of *stomach* which is accepted without qualms, as when Queen Katherine says of the dead Wolsey: 'He was a man of an unbounded stomach, ever ranking Himself with princes.'

---

[1] It may be amusing to record that a snatch of parody offered by Press to illustrate his points was subsequently developed as followed by Mr J. D. McIntosh in *The Spectator*, 21 October 1955:

> In Bakerloo did Aly Khan
> A stately Hippodrome decree:
> Where Alf the bread delivery man
> Collided with a draper's van
>   While doing sixty-three.
> So half a mile of tidy ground
> With cakes and clothes was littered round:
> And here were undies white with gorgeous frills,
> Which brought on many a manly blush to see,
> And here were rock-cakes ancient as the hills,
> Enfolding sundry lots of masonry.
> But oh! that deep traumatic scar which slanted
> Down Alf's left cheek, that whisker could not cover!
> 'A horrid trace; as ugly and unwanted
> As e'er upon a human face was planted
> By Fortune!' said the surgeon, Mr Glover.

VII

The consideration of pairs like *dog* and *bitch*, *guts* and *courage* suggests another concept which is emphasized in the structural approach: the notion of marked and unmarked members, especially of a contrasting relationship.[1] It has, of course, long been recognized that many kinds of signalling or communication are reducible to binary contrasts: yes and no, on and off, plus and minus, high and low. Morse and the inventors of modern computers have this much in common, that they reduce signalling to unambiguous systems of binary contrasts—dot and dash in Morse's code, zero and one in electronic computers. And linguists have long sought to envisage phonological contrasts in terms of binary sets, their attempts being to this extent endorsed by the recent research on 'distinctive features' already referred to. Mr Catford has more to say on this below.

Now, in these binary oppositions, it is common to find one member regarded as more neutral or more normal than the other: the contrast is relatively *unmarked* in one member and relatively *marked* in the other; in other words, the polarity is not equal between the opposing pairs. This is a matter of signalling convenience. When we learn mathematics, we are taught that all numbers are positive or negative, all plus or minus. But for convenience, we do not indicate the contrast between the two sets equally; negative numbers are always prefixed by the minus sign, but unless special circumstances dictate, we omit the plus sign in front of positive numbers. Minus, we may say, is the marked member of the contrast, plus is the unmarked. In London there is a contrast between two types of bus-stop: those at which buses always stop, without reference to the needs of passengers on a specific occasion, and those on the other hand at

[1] Among recent illuminating references to the concept in linguistics, one might mention C. E. Bazell, *Linguistic Form* (Istanbul, 1953), p. 29; F. T. Visser, 'The Terms "Subjunctive" and "Indicative"', *English Studies*, vol. 36 (1955); A. Martinet, 'Linguistique structurale et grammaire comparée', *Travaux de l'Institut de Linguistique*, vol. 1 (1956).

which buses stop only on specific request from inside or outside the bus. In this contrast, the compulsory stop is the unmarked member, signs reading simply *Bus Stop*; the other is the marked member and the signs read *Request Bus Stop*. I mentioned above that marking was a matter of convenience: that is to say, it is related to signalling economy or is conventional. The fact that it is without 'real' significance is illustrated by the situation with bus-stops in Copenhagen, where the same contrast obtains as in London but where the marking is the other way round: *Stoppested* and *Faststoppested* (that is, 'they stop' versus 'they *have to* stop').

The marking of a member in linguistic oppositions can be seen at several levels of English structure, and observation of it provides a valuable insight into the operation of the language. One may instance the inflexional level. English is historically a two-tense language, present versus past: present is, as it were, the natural form of the verb, general and unmarked, and it is in contrast with a morphologically marked form, past, which is specific and particular. But we have long since developed various other means of indicating temporal and aspectual relations, and each of the original forms is now the unmarked member of another contrast: 'simple present' in contrast with 'continuous', the marked form, in one opposition, and in contrast with a specific future indicator in another contrast. 'First, *I do* this; watch me, *I'm doing* it for your benefit.' 'When *you come, you will see* for yourself.' The 'simple past' is the unmarked member of a contrast with a 'past continuous' in one opposition, and with a 'pluperfect' in another. The concept of marked and unmarked helps to explain, for example, how the simple tense can frequently serve to express both a simple and a more complex tense relationship, whereas a complex form (say, the pluperfect) cannot similarly serve the double purpose. Consider the utterance *I saw him after I saw you*, where the second *saw* functions in a position where the corresponding marked form *had seen* would also be idiomatic but is not essential. So, too, the simple past can often function as the (marked) continuous form, but rarely the converse: 'I wrote the letter in a flash of anger.' 'I wrote the letter while the baby cried.' 'I was writing the letter while the baby was crying.' As with the bus-stops, the polarity of the marking here is conventional and is not specially correlated with reality; the determination of the marked forms is a fortuitous result of English linguistic history. In a similar opposition in Russian the polarity is diametrically different from that in the English one: *pisal*, the unmarked form, corresponding to the English marked one, *was writing*; *napisal*, morphologically marked, corresponding to *wrote*.

During an important period in the history of standard English, *thou* and *you* were in contrast, not as singular and plural, but as marked and unmarked members respectively of an opposition with reference to the singular. *You* was the neutral form, of wide application; *thou* was the particularized form used in special contexts and for special effect, whether it was friendly familiarity, cool contempt, or angry scorn. But *thou* normally carried the mark, while *you* did so only when it was used in deliberate contrast to *thou* (for example, in a context where *thou* was the reasonably expected form). Modern French and German, of course, have similar contrasts with similar polarities.

Many excellent examples of this opposition can be seen in exchanges between Shakespeare's characters: indeed, a great deal is lost to the modern reader of Lear's speeches to his daughters or of the banter between Maria, Sir Toby, and Sir Andrew if one is not fully sensitive to the opposition and its implications. But the contrast can scarcely be better illustrated than by a passage in the *Oxford Book of English Talk* reporting the trial in 1603 of Sir Walter Raleigh.[1] Raleigh regularly addresses the Attorney-General, Sir Edward Coke, with the neutral form *you*. And this is shown to be a neutral, unmarked form and not a specifically polite one by its being used a good deal also in Coke's addresses to Raleigh—and it is very plain that Coke has no intention of being polite, even in sarcasm: 'Thou art a monster; thou hast an English face, but a Spanish heart. Now you must have money.' Here we see Coke slip from the marked, the angry

[1] Ed. J. Sutherland (Oxford, 1953), pp. 83 ff, especially p. 85.

and insulting form, to the neutral, general-purpose one which is used in the ordinary course of the prosecution, as in 'Further, you sent to him by your trusty Francis Kemish.' Yet in his immediately following speech (very significantly, when he is trying to make Raleigh lose his temper and so prejudice himself), he says: 'All that he did was by thy instigation, thou viper—for I *thou* thee, thou traytor.'

At the lexical level again there is much evidence of structural contrasts operating with marked and unmarked members, and the importance of being aware of them came home to me when a student repeated in an essay the witticism, 'When Shaw was ninety years young', but could not explain why it was witty. We have several sets of common words which pattern in opposing pairs, like *old* and *young* or *high* and *low*, each readily calling up its antonym. The interest of such bipolar words for semantic research is reflected in a good deal of fruitful work recently undertaken by psychologists,[1] but it is important to realize that the antonymous polarity is often sharply different as between the members, one of a pair being the unmarked member in the opposition and consequently capable of operating outside it. When we say that a person is *old*, we are making a statement in direct relative opposition to saying that he is *young*, but we can ask 'How old is he?' without committing ourselves to expecting him to be relatively old or relatively young; the unmarked character of *old* is seen similarly in statements like 'he is ninety years old' and 'he is two years old'. On the other hand, *young* is the marked member of the contrasting pair and can be put into such collocations only by a deliberate distortion of English semantic structure for a special purpose. There are similar polarities with other pairs. 'How heavy is your piano?' is a neutral inquiry, whereas 'How light is your piano?' gives a special twist to the question: the piano will have to be fairly light for what the speaker has in mind. Compare 'How big is your son?'

[1] See the articles by C. M. Solley and C. J. Messick in *The American Journal of Psychology*, vol. 70 (1957), pp. 161–73, 586–93, and above all C. E. Osgood, G. J. Suci, P. H. Tannenbaum, *The Measurement of Meaning* (Urbana, 1957).

with 'How small is your son?' The latter again raises a special issue; the speaker will perhaps go on to ask if the boy could crawl through the fence to recover a ball.

With the pair *man* and *woman*, the marking is indicated morphologically, as with *lion* and *lioness* and as with the plurals of nouns in contrast with their singulars. The word *man* operates in a number of semantic contrasts. It may mean 'male over the age of twenty-one', in contrast with *minor*; more vaguely, it means 'adult male', in contrast with *boy*; figuratively—by singling out a characteristic of many men—it operates in opposition to *coward* ('Be a man!'); and it can mean 'adult male', in contrast with the morphologically marked form *woman*. In all these oppositions, *man* is the unmarked member of the contrasting pair, and so we find it used not infrequently subsuming the marked members, when it is applied to humanity as a whole, in contrast with non-humanity: 'man and beast'; 'so long as men can breathe or eyes can see'. In some Germanic languages, as once in English, this same characteristic shows in the use of *man* as an indefinite pronoun.[1]

It seems likely that this structural notion of marked and unmarked members of opposing pairs can be applied cautiously but with profit to many of the binary choices in usage at more complex linguistic levels than the lexical. We may well develop a more valid and mature attitude to problems of correctness and incorrectness, propriety and impropriety of expression, by viewing the choices in such a light. Professor Ullmann has suggested in his *Style in the French Novel* that one of the four principles of stylistic explanation is deviation from the norm, and he shows how the choice of word-order with French adjectives can involve something like a marking by position (*une importante découverte, la banale résignation*), since placing the adjective before the noun

---

[1] The male components in opposing pairs are often the unmarked members (*doctor—lady doctor; horse—mare; Lehrer—Lehrerin*), but not always; compare *nurse* and *male-nurse*, *goose* and *gander*, *cow* and *bull* ('daddy-cow'), and others. Nor is marking permanent; note the semantic history of *meat* and *food*; *fowl* and *bird*; *deer, beast,* and *animal*.

enables one to express not only the adjective's lexical meaning but in addition some special emphasis or personal involvement or irony or poetic-archaic flavour.[1]

The Prague School notion of what has been translated as 'foregrounding' brings us close to this too; it is defined by Mukařovský as 'the aesthetically intentional distortion of the linguistic components' in relation to the normal standard language on the one hand and to 'the traditional aesthetic canon' on the other.[2] Thus in English, certain word-order patterns can be viewed as inconspicuous, neutral, unmarked: 'A man who could pass by a sight as majestic and impressive as this would be dull-spirited.' Others are marked by their deviation from the norm and by their conformity with poetic tradition, so that, although they would be intolerable and stylistically vicious if they were used promiscuously, they convey dignity or other special effect (as in Mr Warburg's second example from Hardy, p. 54) on the right occasion: 'Dull would he be of soul who could pass by A sight so touching in its majesty.'[3]

Although I have been able to do no more than present some outlines and suggestions, enough has perhaps been said to indicate the nature and potentiality of a structural approach to the English language and to English Language teaching. A concept of system and structure can do, and indeed is doing, a great deal to engender an objective and scientific attitude to linguistic usage, and to provide a powerful critical tool for analysing it and for increasing our awareness both of its variety and of the significance of its variations. And if pupils become more proficient in talking about their own language and in reacting intellectually and aesthetically to its use by others, they will in consequence achieve what is generally held to be the basic

[1] Op. cit., pp. 6–9.

[2] P. L. Garvin, *A Prague School Reader* (Washington, D.C., 1955), p. 20.

[3] J. Firbas, in an important recent article, also directs attention to 'the deviation from the grammaticized word-order that creates an emotive effect'; see 'Some Thoughts on the Function of Word-Order in Old and Modern English', in *Sborník Prací Filosofické Fakulty Brněnské University*, vol. 6 (1957), series A, pp. 72–100.

utilitarian end of English teaching, the ability to use it better themselves. But in addition—and we should err seriously if we overlooked this—the structural approach brings us nearer to an understanding of the most characteristic human activity and nearer to linking it up with the rest of man's patterned and systematic behaviour.

CHAPTER 3

Some Aspects of Style | *Jeremy Warburg*

I

'A discussion of the word Style', it has been suggested, 'if it were pursued with only a fraction of the rigour of a scientific investigation, would inevitably cover the whole of literary aesthetics and the theory of criticism. Six books would not suffice for the attempt. . . .'[1] Much less, I should add, will a sixth of a single one.

And yet, this is the word—style—which one so often hears used in conjunction with the word 'mere'—mere style—as if style were a rather poor relation, an appendage of an infinitely richer 'meaning'. That, I suppose, is the result of treating form and content as though they were separate entities, as though we knew the meaning of an utterance by any other way than by the way it had been said. Of course, we do not. As Roger Ascham put it: 'They be not wise, therefore that say, what care I for a mans wordes and utterance, if his matter and reasons be good?'[2] If we modify the way in which an utterance is made, we shall also, necessarily, modify its effect. We may, perhaps, regard this alteration of effect as slight, even as inconsiderable; but, slight or considerable—and, as we shall see, it is very often considerable—it nonetheless exists. Now style—the classification is somewhat

[1] J. Middleton Murry, *The Problem of Style* (Oxford, 1922, edn of 1949), pp. 3 f. I shall in fact limit myself to some discussion of *what*, it seems to me, should be taught about style; and I shall leave to Mr Mittins the task of discussing, among other things, *how* best it may be taught.

[2] *The Scholemaster* (1570), ed. J. E. B. Mayor (London, 1934), p. 180.

arbitrary, like all classifications, but this, I believe, is a valuable one—style seems to me to be involved in only one part of this semantic field: it is not, at the lexical level, for example, concerned with such a radical distinction as that between the use of the terms (say) *night* rather than *day*; it is concerned only with the subtler distinctions of meaning which may be made by choosing one linguistic form rather than others whose denotations are essentially the same, but whose connotations are different. These, however, are by no means distinctions between one or another kind of trivial embellishment: they are effective distinctions between one or another kind of sense.

They are, then, important distinctions—the kind or order of distinction we can make as we choose between the 'tones' of *Your silence is requested*, and *Quiet, please*, and *Would you be so good?* and *Do shut up*, and *Put a sock in it*, and *Drop dead!* They are the kind or order of distinction we are making when we choose between the 'learned' words *oration, identical, conflagration*, and the more 'popular' *speech, same*, and *fire*; between the personal *I will write to you again on Monday* and the impersonal *It is being arranged that you should be further advised on Monday*;[1] between the active *Boys and girls go out to play*, and the passive *Recreation is taken by juveniles in open-air conditions*;[1] between the positive *It is difficult to make people understand*, and the negative *It is a matter of not inconsiderable difficulty to make people understand*; between the 'appreciatory' or 'neutral' *farmer, planter, tiller of the soil*, and the depreciatory (as well as American) *rube, hayseed*, and *hick*.[2]

This is all part of the pool of language on which the English can draw, and it is wonderfully rich: 'neither cann any tongue', said Richard Carew, 'deliver a matter with more varietye than ours, both plainely and by proverbes and Metaphors . . . when wee would be rid of one wee use to saye *Bee going, trudge, pack*,

[1] From R. W. Bell, 'Form, Style and Expression', in *Communication in Industry*, ed. Cecil Chisholm (London, 1955), pp. 82 f. But I question the value of his 'rules'.

[2] Cleanth Brooks and Robert Penn Warren, *Fundamentals of Good Writing* (New York, 1950, London edn of 1952), p. 350.

be faring, hence, awaye, shifte, and, by circumlocution, *rather your roome then your companye, Letts see your backe, com againe when I bid you . . . spare us your place, another in your steede, a shipp of salte for you, save your credite, you are next the doore, the doore is open for you, theres no bodye holdes you, noe bodie teares your sleeve, &c'.*[1] Now, we cannot pretend that these can all be interchanged, regardless of the contexts in which they may occur, without significantly altering the effect: *courage,* as Professor Quirk has pointed out, is not the same as *guts;* and it is not the same as *bravery, fortitude, valour, pluck, spirit,* or *spunk.* For one thing, *courage* is an abstract term, *guts* concrete; for another, *courage* in contrast to *guts* involves a literal use of the term, *guts* in contrast to *courage* a figurative one; then, *guts* has one syllable, and *courage* has two; and, for that matter, they do not rhyme. . . . To put it in a blunt and unpedantic form, they are different words—and that, I have found in practice, is not a superfluous or such a trivial thing to say. For, whether or not their referent is supposed to be the same, their associations are distinct. We need only do a little substitution—*guts* for *courage* in some existing texts—to see how very distinct they can be:

> Now therefore keep they sorrow to thyself, and bear with good guts that which hath befallen thee . . .
>
> (*The Apocrypha*)

> A soft Kentucky strain was in his voice,
> And the Ohio's deeper boom was there,
> With some wild accents of old Wabash days,
>   And winds of Illinois;
> And when he spoke he took us unaware,
> With his high guts and unselfish ways . . .
>
> (Maurice Thompson, 'At Lincoln's Grave')

> But screw your guts to the sticking-place,
> And we'll not fail. . .
>
> (*Macbeth*)

Now I admit that two of these examples, certainly, depend for their incongruity on the intrusion of the literal sense of *guts;*

[1] *The Excellencye of the English Tongue* (?1595–6), in *Elizabethan Critical Essays,* ed. G. Gregory Smith (Oxford, 1904), vol. 2, p. 292.

nevertheless it would not have meant the same, lexically, to have screwed one's *pluck to the sticking-place*, nor, rhythmically (if not lexically), to have screwed one's *fortitude to the sticking-place*. Of course I am not suggesting that there are no two or more words which are in some sense synonymous: I am only suggesting that they are rare.

The good use of a *language*, then, consists in choosing the appropriate symbolization of the experience you wish to convey, from among all the possible words and arrangements of words (by saying, for example, *dog* rather than *cat*). Good *style*, it seems to me, consists in choosing the appropriate symbolization of the experience you wish to convey, from among a number of words *whose meaning-area is roughly, but only roughly, the same* (by saying *cat*, for example, rather than *pussy*). That is say, matters of style are necessarily linguistic matters: linguistic matters are not necessarily—it is a common but misleading view—matters of style.[1]

Further, though stylistic selections, like other kinds of linguistic selection, depend for their success simply on the aptness of their relation to the experiences you wish to convey, they involve subtler discriminations than other kinds of linguistic selection, and, consequently, success in making them is somewhat harder to achieve.

II

Others have taken a more dogmatic point of view.[2] One finds it— at the lexical level, for example—in the work of Quiller-Couch: 'Train your suspicions to bristle up whenever you come upon "as regards", "with regard to", "in respect of". . . . They are all

---

[1] Cf. Stendhal, *Du Style*: 'Le style est ceci: Ajouter à une pensée donnée toutes les circonstances propres à produire tout l'effet que doit produire cette pensée.' (Quoted in Middleton Murry, *The Problem of Style*, p. 79.)

[2] Cf. S. A. Leonard, *The Doctrine of Correctness in English Usage, 1700–1800* (Madison, 1929), especially (p. 244) 'a great part of the prescriptions assembled in this study are still repeated in handbooks and style-sheets and the like today'.

dodges of Jargon, circumlocutions for evading this or that simple statement . . . *you should never use them.*' [1] Or one can find it—at the phonological level—in a review of George Goodwin's 'Rising Castle', in 1799: 'In one of the poems', the reviewer points out, 'the name of a village called *Snettisham*' (pronounced, I believe, *Snetzum*) 'is introduced. We hope', he says, '*never to hear* this unpleasing sound again in verse. If our author will look into the funereal odes of Dr Watts . . . he will see the ridiculous effect produced by the use of ill-sounding proper names.' [2] Now I have to admit, I have never looked into the funereal odes of Dr Watts; but I can quite imagine the ridiculous effect produced by *his particular use* of proper names; and it is true that *Snettisham*, in *the specific context* of Goodwin's poem, may not give a particularly pleasing impression. But there is nothing necessarily unpleasing, ridiculous, or unpoetic about the sound of *Snettisham*; it could, I take it, be used effectively in verse, in much the same way as *Cambridge, Wembley, Harrow-on-the-Hill, Padstow, Pontefract, Leigh-on-Sea, Woodhall Spa, Ruislip, Middlesex, Highgate, Neasden,* and *Willesden Green* can all be used effectively in verse—as, indeed, John Betjeman does use them in his book of poems, *A Few Late Chrysanthemums* (1954).

No less dogmatic is the all-too-common text-book 'rule' which has it that verbal discourse—especially description—*ought to be* concrete. [3] Browning's

> the lowest boughs and the brushwood sheaf
> Round the elm-tree bore are in tiny leaf

is, one would be bound to assert, lexically *better* than *spring's here again*, although no circumstances, or rather, far too many circumstances, are given in such text-books for it to be better in. [4] This is capricious in much the same way as the Fowlers' injunc-

---

[1] *On the Art of Writing* (Cambridge, 1916), p. 94 (my italics).

[2] *The Critical Review*, New Series, vol. 25 (1799), p. 318 (my italics).

[3] Cf. Quiller-Couch, op. cit., pp. 87, 96.

[4] Cf. W. K. Wimsatt, Jr., and M. C. Beardsley, *The Verbal Icon* (University of Kentucky Press, 1954), pp. 133 ff.

tion to 'prefer the Saxon word to the Romance' is capricious [1]—
a precept which even Q regarded as 'false in theory and likely to
be fatal in practice'. [2] And in fact, as the Fowlers themselves were
aware, if you deliberately try to restrict your choice of words to
one or other of these two main ingredients of English vocabulary,
you will merely produce curiosities like this—

Though, for some hundreds of years, English folk—headed by the best
songsters of the land—have been seeking to shake off the Norman yoke that
lies so heavy on their speech, yet what many speakers and writers, even today,
call English is no English at all but sheer French. Nevertheless there are many
who feel not a little ashamed of the needless loan-words in which their speech
is clothed, and of the borrowed feathers in which they strut—

which is 'pure Saxon'; or like this—

Despite the fact that during several centuries English people—captained by
the chief poets of the country—have attempted to escape the Norman yoke
which exerts so ponderous a constraint on their language, the idiom many
orators and literary people, even at present, style English, is by no means
English, but purely French. Despite this, numerous individuals are considerably abashed by the unnecessary adopted terms in which their language is
dressed and the alien plumes in which they parade—

which, though denotatively the same as the passage before it, is
(almost) 'pure Romance'. [3]

Critics such as these, then, make no attempt to define precisely,
often fail even to ascertain, the purpose of a particular utterance
and its context-of-situation; and they recommend over-simplified
and sometimes superfluous devices for achieving the very general
purposes which they prescribe. They tend to presuppose, consciously or unconsciously, and to a greater or lesser degree, that

[1] *The King's English*, 2nd edn (Oxford, 1906), p. 1.

[2] Op. cit., p. 138.

[3] Both passages are taken from Stanley Rundle's *Language as a Social and
Political Factor in Europe* (London, 1946), pp. 32 f. The first is itself a quotation
from Charles Dessoulavy's *The Word-book of the English Tongue* (London, 1917),
which, as Rundle says, 'advocated the sole use of the Saxon part of our language without its Norman-French superstructure'. These passages, and some
of the other material used in this paper, have appeared in my article, 'The
Best-Chosen Language', in *Impulse*, May 1958, to whose editors I am grateful
for permission to reprint.

there is a one-and-only proper form for verbal discourse.[1] This is as if one claimed that Richardson was just a less efficient kind of Sterne, and it is equally absurd. Or, as Tennyson put it, 'to decry one original poet' (or, I should add, one original speaker or writer in any other kind) 'in order to magnify another is like despising an oak-tree because you prefer a beech, and almost as sensible.'[2]

But these are the foundations on which many people build calculating that a style is intrinsically 'bad' if it does not conform to the despotism of their personal linguistic tastes. It seems to me that the rooms in these buildings have at best a sadly restricted and at worst an absurdly distorted view. For example, as Professor C. S. Lewis has pointed out so well,

Nearly all our older poetry was written and read by men to whom the distinction between poetry and rhetoric, in its modern form, would have been meaningless. The 'beauties' which they chiefly regarded in every composition were those which we either dislike or simply do not notice. . . . Probably all our literary histories . . . are vitiated by our lack of sympathy on this point . . . we must reconcile ourselves to the fact that of the praise and censure which we allot to medieval and Elizabethan poets only the smallest part would have seemed relevant to those poets themselves.[3]

We should reconcile ourselves to the fact that we too often condemn a technique merely because we are out of sympathy with the experience—the pleasure, perhaps, of an intricate and dexterous pattern, simply *of form itself*, of verbal gymnastics—which the technique was intended to convey. We should reconcile ourselves to the fact that there is no one style which is better, regardless of the circumstances, than another; but that there are styles which gratify particular needs more adequately than others.[4] Of course, one may regard the need itself formulated by

[1] See, for example, F. L. Lucas's *Style* (London, 1955). But, though I profoundly disagree with the principles on which it is based, I am indebted to it for a number of the examples, not specifically acknowledged, which I have used.

[2] Hallam Tennyson, *Alfred Lord Tennyson: a Memoir* (London, 1897), vol. 2, p. 349.

[3] *English Literature in the Sixteenth Century* (Oxford, 1954), p. 61.

[4] Cf. Randolph Quirk, '"Dialects" within Standard English', *Transactions of the Yorkshire Dialect Society*, pt. 58, vol. 10 (1958), pp. 29–42.

a given style—the wish (let us say) to talk of cabbages, and not of kings, the wish to misrepresent or swear—as either trivial or perverse; but that is a matter of philosophical or ethical, and not of technical, concern. Techniques should be judged, not in terms of the 'goodness' or 'badness' of the experiences which they convey, but simply in terms of their effectiveness as methods of conveying them.

III

Rhythms, then, 'may be harsh and abrupt or lingering and subtle. Diction'—and here I am primarily concerned with the lexical level of language, and primarily with the literal usage of that—'diction may be homely and direct or elaborate and suggestive. Sentence structure may be simple and downright or complicated by modifying and qualifying elements. Appeal may be made through logic or through persuasion.'[1] These and many other factors are related to the speaker's or writer's conception of the relationships between himself, the subject, and the hearer or reader. Mrs Gaskell has told us how careful Charlotte Brontë, for example, was about her choice of words: 'One set of words was the truthful mirror of her thoughts; no others, however apparently identical in meaning, would do. . . . She would wait patiently, searching for the right term, until it presented itself to her. It might be provincial, it might be derived from the Latin; so that it accurately represented her idea, she did not mind whence it came. . . . She never wrote down a sentence until she clearly understood what she wanted to say, had deliberately chosen the words, and arranged them in their right order.'[2]

[1] Brooks and Warren, op. cit., p. 6. We are accustomed to the idea of a connexion between the choice of *words* and the meanings conveyed; but we are far less accustomed to the idea of a connexion between the choice of *arrangements* and the meanings conveyed. *Chewing his finger-nails, Sammy came in* does not mean *Sammy came in chewing his finger-nails*. 'Soul' (says Dr Lucas, op. cit., p. 49) 'is more than syntax.' No doubt; but syntax may well illuminate the soul.

[2] E. C. Gaskell, *The Life of Charlotte Brontë* (London, 1857, edn of 1906), p. 235.

One should decide what it is, then, in a distinct situation, that one wishes to convey. Perhaps, an impression of homeliness. In this case, one should use words and arrangements of words which have what are regarded as 'homely' associations. This is not only important, it is obvious as well—sufficiently obvious to be often overlooked. They may, quite incidentally, be 'Saxon' and concrete; and then again, they may not. There are so many exceptions which do not prove the homely-simple Saxon 'rule'; besides, how many people are well enough acquainted with the etymologies of words to make selections in this way—even if it were desirable they should?

Or, again, if one considers it necessary to give an impression of civility rather than of brusqueness, one should use (in conjunction, perhaps, with certain gestures and facial expressions) words and arrangements of words whose connotations are regarded as civil rather than as brusque: *Would you please be good enough to send the money?* rather than *Send the money, quick.* Or, if you find it more effective, *We should be obliged for a prompt remittance.* . . . Of course, it is customary to deplore that sort of style.[1] It is not, say its critics, 'good, plain English'; it is not, they say, the kind of English which Civil Servants, for example, ought to use.[2] Now I wonder to what extent that is true. 'Good, plain English' is by no means compatible with *every* kind of experience which a civil servant is obliged to convey; and perhaps it is not even compatible with the majority of experiences which *certain* civil servants are obliged to convey. They may find it necessary to use, not one, but several dialects. Some time ago, a friend of mine wrote to a certain branch of this Service, complaining of the jargon, the gobbledygook-style, of a letter requesting payment which they had sent him. This was part of their answer to his criticism: 'Your criticisms are appreciated but experience over many years has demonstrated that any wording less formal

---

[1] Cf. Quiller-Couch, *On the Art of Writing*, p. 94.

[2] Cf. Sir Ernest Gowers' *Plain Words* (London, 1948). Gowers, of course, mentions some (if only some) of the limitations of his book: many of those who read it (and many of those who merely hear of it) are not aware of them.

than that used would not be as effective.' Surely that must be very often true.[1] Of course, a pile of manure by any other name will *smell* exactly as it had smelt before, but there would certainly be people who thought that it *sounded* more, or less, pleasing. And those sales campaigns, for example, in which the proverbial spade—whether it is a good, a bad, or an indifferent spade—is simply called a spade, will not necessarily be as successful as those which are conducted in more sophistical ways: *toilet roll*, people may feel, is somehow 'nicer' than *lavatory paper*, but, if that is what they feel, it is not because the article referred to—the thing itself—is 'nicer', but, for them (temporarily at least), the symbols which express it. At any rate, it may be thought necessary to sweeten the referential pill; it may be thought necessary to flex the verbal muscles of authority. In the words of Lewis Carroll:

> Then, if you'd be impressive,
> Remember what I say,
> That abstract qualities begin
> With capitals alway:
> The Good, the True, the Beautiful,—
> Those are the things that pay!

Indeed, 'authority', or 'sweetness' (or, for that matter, 'I am speaking'), may be virtually all that a given utterance means, and all that it is intended to mean. 'Plainness'—a very vague term, of course, but one by which people generally mean a clear and logical use of the language, facilitated, from a linguistic point of view, by using mostly short and familiar words and arrangements of words—'plainness', even where it may be possible, may not always be desirable; neither you, nor, indeed, your audience, may regard it as effective. Mistiness, said Newman, is the mother of safety; and, I should add, there are plenty of people who are enormously impressed by it: 'I watna, sir,' said a beadle when his opinion of a sermon was asked, 'it was rather

---

[1] It was 'one of the principles of the Circumlocution Office never, on any account whatever, to give a straightforward answer' (Dickens, *Little Dorrit*). This is no less, but it is also, of course, *little more* unsound, as a stylistic principle, than that of *always* giving a straightforward answer.

o'er-plain and simple for me. I like thae sermons bae that joombles the joodgement and confounds the sense.'[1] And Captain Cuttle, you may recall, tended to estimate the value of Bunsby's opinions 'in proportion to the immensity of the difficulty he experienced in making anything out of them'.[2]

IV

What, exactly, we should ask ourselves, do we wish to convey? for, as Montaigne put it, 'to him that knoweth not the port to which he is bound no wind can be favourable; neither can he who has not yet determined at what mark he is to shoot direct his arrow aright'. For example, the scientific mark, the mark of a strictly scientific presentation, is the very small bull's-eye of a 'pure' denotation—one word, one precise and (ideally) unalterable sense; and a 'scientific' style (which is no more the prerogative of science than an 'artistic' style is the prerogative of art) is as rigidly objective as it can be, and, incidentally, the farthest-removed from the norm of colloquial speech.[3] The phrase *Green grow the rushes oh!* would merely be regarded as un-apt by someone who had reason to expect a strictly scientific statement. The pleasant or unpleasant associations which the phrase might evoke he would regard, quite rightly, as irrelevant.[4] What, he might ask, is the point of the inversion? What is the purpose of the *oh*? (Or why, for that matter, quote a traditional song?) Besides, from the point of view of a strictly scientific presentation, the statement is vague; for what species of rushes are these? In a scientific context, then, *Green grow the rushes oh!* is wrong, and *Juncus conglomeratus is green* is right. And, as Mr Brookes points out (p. 134), to the scientist statements such as these 'can be original, creative, imaginative, profound, elegant, in precisely the same aesthetic sense as these words are used by

[1] Lucas, *Style*, p. 74.   [2] Dickens, *Dombey and Son*.

[3] Samples of colloquial speech, and a discussion of its characteristics, will be found in Randolph Quirk's 'Colloquial English and Communication', *Studies in Communication*, ed. B. Ifor Evans (London, 1955), pp. 169–82.

[4] Cf. Brooks and Warren, op. cit., pp. 32 f.

the man of letters'. As *Ripeness is all* is to one, so *Energy is conserved if heat is taken into account* is to the other.

The legal style *par excellence* is also the result of a desire to be as nearly unambiguous as one can; which is not, unfortunately, and very often cannot be, the same as being easily understood. The lawyer, when he is dealing with the law, must 'not be afraid of repetitions, or even of identifying them by *aforesaids*; he must limit by definition words with a penumbra dangerously large, and amplify with a string of near-synonyms words with a penumbra dangerously small; he must eschew all pronouns when their antecedents might possibly be open to dispute, and generally avoid every potential grammatical ambiguity'.[1] The following example is symptomatic of such desires:

In the Nuts (Unground) (Other than Groundnuts) Order, the expression nuts shall have reference to such nuts, other than groundnuts, as would, but for this Amending Order, not qualify as nuts (Unground) (Other than Groundnuts) by reason of their being nuts (Unground).[2]

Now this may bring you to laughter and despair; but, in a legal context, there is really no alternative—that is the law. The language used is, in fact, 'a complete economic adjustment of means to an end, and more than this we cannot ask of any man's language'.[3] Less, in the circumstances, may be troublesome, and possibly disastrous.[4]

One could add almost indefinitely to these examples of styles which, of their kind, seem to have been appropriately used; but I

[1] Gowers, *Plain Words*, p. 7, with reference to Dr Glanville Williams's 'Language and the Law', *Law Quarterly Review*, vol. 61 (April 1945).

[2] Quoted in Randolph Quirk, '"Dialects" within Standard English', *Transactions of the Yorkshire Dialect Society*, pt. 58, vol. 10 (1958), p. 32.

[3] G. P. Krapp, 'Standards of Speech and their Values', *Modern Philology*, vol. 11 (1913), p. 67.

[4] Not long ago, for example, the phrase *Please Take a Basket* was inscribed on a notice in a supermarket. A woman took one home, and returned for another a week or two later; she was arrested, tried, and found *not guilty*. 'Why shouldn't someone take one?' as the judge observed. The notice in the supermarket was removed.

will only add two. There is this (from Brooks and Warren, op. cit., p. 393), of an advertising kind:

It's Listerine, for you chum. . . . but *quick*! Those innocent-looking flakes and scales you see on scalp, hair or dress-shoulders, are a warning. . . . This is no time to fool around with smelly lotions or sticky salves that can't kill germs. You need antiseptic action . . . and you need it quick.

Chum, it will be noticed, not *friend*; *quick*, not *quickly*; *smelly*, not *scented*; *can't* not *cannot* or *are unable to*. And the use that has been made of alliteration and asyndeton will also be noticed. All of this was presumably intended to give an impression, to reinforce an idea, of urgency, danger, and bonhomie—that is, the appropriate conditions for a sale. Not for every kind of sale—'the kid glove', one agency executive has been reported as saying, 'can also pack a brick'—but, apparently, for this particular commodity at that particular time.

And there is this example, of a journalistic kind, in a report of the fight which took place between the giant Italian Carnera and the Negro Joe Louis in June 1935. You will notice how few opportunities for antonomastic variation have been missed:

The frozen-faced, sloe-eyed Negro's defeat of Carnera was enacted before 57,000 pairs of eyes red with blood lust. . . . The imperturbable brown bear . . . had whanged away under Carnera's guard . . . until the jittery giant had become very weary indeed. . . . The sensational Senegambian was pinned in a corner . . . the lad with the petrified puss was upon Carnera as he rose as wobbly as a punch-drunk fighter on stilts. . . . Crack, crack! went the right and left of this calmly savage Ethiopian to the head of the battered derelict. . . . He feinted with his hands and the vast Venetian threw up his hands widely as his wits scattered.[1]

Now Quiller-Couch, I may say, would not have liked it.[2] This entertaining and illuminating habit of having two (or three, or four, or five) shies at the coconut for the price of one, did not apparently appeal to him at all. And of course there are contexts in which the use of this device will be more difficult, even impossible, to justify—in prose, for example, intended to have a

[1] Quoted in Wimsatt and Beardsley, *The Verbal Icon*, pp. 192 f.
[2] Cf. *On the Art of Writing*, p. 93.

more logical appeal. But, as Professor Wimsatt has implied, this is by no means an inappropriate mode for, among other things, the popular bardic reporting of heroic conflict in the twentieth century;[1] and this particular passage is, in its particular place and way, it seems to me, quite admirable.

V

Generally, the speaker or writer, in conveying what he wants to convey, also wants, as best he can, to make a good impression on a certain audience—on others, that is, besides himself. Anthony Trollope did, for one; referring to *The Last Chronicle of Barset*, he wrote in his *Autobiography*:

I was sitting one morning at work upon the novel at the end of the long drawing-room of the Athenaeum Club . . . As I was there, two clergymen . . . seated themselves . . . close to me. They soon began to abuse what they were reading, and each was reading some part of some novel of mine. The gravamen of their complaint lay in the fact that I reintroduced the same character so often! 'Here,' said one, 'is that archdeacon whom we have had in every novel he has ever written.' 'And here,' said the other, 'is the old duke whom he has talked about till everybody is tired of him. If I could not invent new characters, I would not write novels at all.' Then one of them fell foul of Mrs Proudie. It was impossible for me not to hear their words, and almost impossible to hear them and be quiet. I got up, and standing between them, I acknowledged myself to be the culprit. 'As to Mrs Proudie,' I said, 'I will go home and kill her before the week is over.' And so I did.

Now Mrs Proudie is far from being a linguistic form; but, in the first place, I did not want to miss the opportunity of repeating the story if I could, and in the second, Mrs Proudie *is*, after all, a form of experience, and the repetition (or, in this case, the omission) of Mrs Proudie is analogous to the repetition or omission of any other kind of form in a particular composition. At any rate, almost all the examples I have quoted so far, satisfy, more or less equally, the 'demands' of the 'sayer' and of the 'sayee' (in Samuel Butler's terms) in relation to the subject concerned; and it would not be difficult at all to find rather more

---

[1] Wimsatt and Beardsley, op. cit., p. 193.

'literary' parallels. Most of the great prose-writers (as Professor Grierson has pointed out[1]), from Hooker to Milton and Clarendon, were, we know and we can tell, scholars writing for scholars —hence their 'latinized' vocabulary and their Ciceronian periods, as well as their quotations and allusions. The blend of racy, colloquial-sounding English and 'euphuistic' artifice in the writings of the University Wits of the Elizabethan age was intended—as we know and can tell—for the young and sophisticated man-about-town, who knew his classical background fairly well and his contemporary Italian or Italianate literature still better. Wyclif, Latimer, and Bunyan, on the other hand, were dealing with a far less educated audience, and consequently their technique is concerned with making far less complicated effects— which is not the same as saying that it is an easier technique.

But of course, as I have implied, the sayer may not find it possible, or desirable, to make a good impression on a given audience. He may, for example, say *chips* in the *Jardin des Gourmets*, and *pommes frites* in the local café. He may be obliged by the unfamiliar or distasteful nature of the experience he wishes to convey, to convey it in what may be regarded, at any rate at first, as an unfamiliar or distasteful way. Joyce, unlike Scott, did not consult his sales-returns to see exactly what the public liked. This is not intended as a slur on Scott; it is simply that Joyce did not find it possible (at least in *Finnegans Wake*) to satisfy an immediate public (or to satisfy much of that public) without, in relation to the experience which he wished to convey, compromising his integrity. Ibsen's *Peer Gynt* is another case in point. If *Peer Gynt* was not the Norwegian idea of poetry, said Ibsen, then it was going to become so. A number of professional writers, many of them little regarded at first, but whom we now regard as great, have felt bound to create an extraordinary, a peculiarly personal, manner to convey, as exactly as possible, the nature of their experience—men, as Dostoevsky's Raskolnikov put it, 'who have the gift or the talent to utter *a new word*'.

[1] H. J. C. Grierson, *Rhetoric and English Composition* (Edinburgh, 1944), pp. 16 f.

But these are the rare exceptions—and (as I say) they are usually professional literary men—rather than the rule. Most people are not professional literary men, let alone professional literary men of a particularly original turn of mind. Most of us, whether speaking or writing, are predisposed more to the methods of Herodotus, who packed his history in a portmanteau, carted it to Olympia, found a favourable pitch, and wooed his audience like any Hyde Park orator.[1] At any rate, though Britannia may quite often waive the rules, there are certain rules which one can only waive at the risk of permanent unintelligibility. Even Joyce, though he is often very difficult to understand, is probably never incomprehensible. I suspect that he always conforms, at least at the morphological level, to the fundamental patterns of English (or Irish, or Latin, or French).

But obviously, in cases of this kind, like Joyce's, it may be hard—certainly at first—to make an assessment of the style, to decide whether or not it is conveying the experience it is intended to convey in the most efficient way; simply because we cannot be sure that we have understood the experience. It may be that we are unable or unwilling to understand; or it may be that the sayer is unable or unwilling, so far as we or, perhaps, so far as anyone else is concerned, to make himself understood. The sayer, perhaps, may be indulging in what the Mock Turtle called 'Reeling and Writhing . . . and the different branches of Arithmetic—Ambition, Distraction, Uglification, and Derision'. In *Kwannon* (the quotation is taken from an art-catalogue),

a title which has religious overtones, the linear form weaving around a central void, is, from one point of view, a series of interlocked rectangles animating the contained and interpenetrated space, and from another is a meditation on the idea of the void in which all oppositions of the world illusion (which is also real) are reconciled. . . .

Now the passage may be relevant to *Kwannon* and significant as an explanation of *Kwannon*, and the writer may not have regarded it as possible to write what he wanted to write about *Kwannon* in any other way. But the passage may possibly relate to,

[1] Quiller-Couch, op. cit., p. 44.

and be significant as an explanation of, primarily the writer of the 'explanation'. We might, in fact, decide that the style is inadequate as an expression of the *overt* purpose of the passage (to convey information about *Kwannon* which could, without over-simplification, have been conveyed more simply), and therefore, from this point of view, that it is 'bad'; but we might also decide that it is admirably serving some *covert* purpose which the writer had in mind (to convey misleading information about *Kwannon*, and, for that matter, certain information about himself), and therefore, from this point of view, that it is 'good'. In fact, various forms of propaganda are undoubtedly 'good' in this sense. You probably remember what Disraeli's Taper and Tadpole said when they were trying to think of a suitable slogan for an electioneering campaign:

> 'Ancient institutions and modern improvements, I suppose, Mr Tadpole.'
> 'Ameliorations is the better word; ameliorations. Nobody knows exactly what it means.'[1]

Unethical? No doubt. But it would be absurd to condemn eating because some men are greedy, or drinking because some men are drunkards, or sex because some men are adulterers; and it would be equally absurd to condemn rhetoric because some men are sophists. It is, in other words, no condemnation of an art that it may be abused.[2]

---

[1] Disraeli, *Coningsby*. Cf. Dickens, *Great Expectations*: Mrs Gargery 'laughed and nodded her head a great many times, and even repeated after Biddy, the words "Pip" and "Property". But I doubt if they had more meaning in them than an election cry, and I cannot suggest a darker picture of her state of mind.'

[2] Cf. *The Rhetoric of Aristotle*, tr. R. C. Jebb (Cambridge, 1909), pp. 4 f. (1355*b*). That, as I say, does not preclude one from criticising what is expressed by art. Far from it. ' "The important thing," says my interviewer, "seems to me to be not the rightness of Strindberg's belief, but rather how he has expressed it. . . ." Strindberg expressed it very vividly, but there are things more important than that. If a man tells me something I believe to be an untruth, am I forbidden to do more than congratulate him on the brilliance of his lying?' (Kenneth Tynan, 'Ionesco and the Phantom', *The Observer*, 6 July 1958, p. 15.) Certainly not. One must simply discriminate between criticisms of a technical and criticisms of a non-technical kind.

VI

In fact, bad style should only be said to consist in failing to give the impression you want to give, either because you do not know the appropriate conventions or because you have failed to apply them. It reveals itself in the use of *more* words than you need to give the impression you want to give, or in the use of *fewer* words than you need to give the impression you want to give, or in the use of words with *other connotations* than you need to give the impression you want to give.

The last, of course, involves some degree of incongruity. Either wholly or in part a style may not be compatible with the purpose (so far as we know it) and the circumstances of a given utterance. There is a passage in Mr E. M. Forster's *Howards End* which illuminates this point particularly well:

Leonard was trying to form his style on Ruskin: he understood him to be the greatest master of English Prose. He read forward steadily, occasionally making a few notes.

'Let us consider a little each of these characters in succession, and first (for of the shafts enough has been said already), what is very peculiar to this church —its luminousness.'

Was there anything to be learnt from this fine sentence? Could he adapt it to the needs of daily life? Could he introduce it, with modifications, when he next wrote a letter to his brother, the lay-reader? For example:

'Let us consider a little each of these characters in succession, and first (for of the absence of ventilation enough has been said already), what is very peculiar to this flat—its obscurity.'

Something told him that the modifications would not do; and that something, had he known it, was the spirit of English Prose. 'My flat is dark as well as stuffy.' Those were the words for him.

'Those were the words for him.' So Hardy thought it necessary to emend the phrase in his *Poems of 1912–13*,

> By this spot where, calmly quite,
> She informed me what would happen by and by . . .

to

> By this spot where, calmly quite,
> She unfolded what would happen by and by . . .

presumably because he felt that *informed* was too prosaic and formal a word in the context of this particular poem. And he emended another of the *Poems of 1912–13* in much the same way, altering

> Yet the fact indeed remains the same
> You are past love, praise, indifference, blame.

to

> Yet abides the fact, indeed, the same
> You are past love, praise, indifference, blame.[1]

We may not regard the substitutions as much of an improvement —here, as Mr McDowall observes, the emended form is rather worse than the original (really the trouble lies in *fact*, not in *remains* at all)—but we can readily understand the reasons which prompted the inversion, and his use of the word *abides*.

Puttenham objected to a translation of Virgil which had it 'that Aeneas was fayne to trudge out of Troy'. This, he said, was 'better to be spoken of a beggar, or of a rogue, or a lackey'. Juno, he insisted, should not 'tugge' at Aeneas.[2] It was, for Puttenham, a carter's word, connoting oxen and horses, or boys pulling at one another's ears: too low a word for such a high occasion, indecorous for such a noble character, and one, presumably, that conveyed an impression which the translator did not want to convey. Of course, the classification of styles into

---

[1] Quoted in Arthur McDowall, *Thomas Hardy* (London, 1931), pp. 242 f. In fact, emendations provide some of the most instructive material for students of style. See, for example, A. F. Scott, *The Poet's Craft* (Cambridge, 1957). Also of interest in this respect is a manuscript version of Arnold Bennett's *A Man from the North*, copiously annotated by the author, in the Ogden Library at University College London.

[2] *The Arte of English Poesie* (?1585), ed. Gladys Willcock and Alice Walker (Cambridge, 1936), pp. 273 f. As Somerset Maugham puts it, echoing a long rhetorical tradition: 'And just as behaviour should proceed from character so should speech. A fashionable woman should talk like a fashionable woman, a street walker like a street walker, a soda jerker like a soda jerker and a lawyer like a lawyer.' ('What Makes a Good Novel Great', *New York Times Book Review*, 30 November 1947, p. 1.) Or—as a distinguished Justice has been reported as saying—'customers in bars do not talk like Chancery Division barristers'.

high, middle, and low—which used to be the rule in manuals and hand-books of rhetoric—is less appropriate to a society in which the 'lines' between aristocracy, bourgeoisie, and working class are far less readily discerned; but we should not normally wish to give the impression that Queens speak Cockney or Cockneys the Queen's English; and it is, indeed, mixtures of this sort which make for the more piquant forms of bathos. Boswell has mentioned the explosion of mirth which greeted the reading of one of the passages from Grainger's poem, *The Sugar-Cane* (1759), at Reynolds' house. It occurred when he read the apostrophe, *Now, Muse, let's sing of rats*. . . . There is no reason to think that they were laughing at the thing itself—the rattiness of rats; Virgil, after all, has successfully versified dung, Dyer sheep, Cowper cucumbers; and, as George Orwell has pointed out, 'the truly remarkable thing about' Joyce's '*Ulysses* . . . is the commonplaceness of its material'.[1] No: it was primarily the word, the form itself—*rats* in such a close proximity to *Muse*—which made them laugh. At any rate, the phrase was not included in the printed version of the poem, and the 'rats', where they appear, are more 'elegantly' named:

> Nor with less waste the whisker'd vermin race,
> A countless clan, despoil the low-land cane.

There was nothing about that to offend contemporary poetic tastes. In fact, there was nothing about the poem as a whole to offend contemporary poetic tastes—it was perfectly well received.[2] We today may not like it, but then, we do not have the same poetic tastes. We may feel that the proper impression of 'fish', in poetry, is conveyed by *fish*: for many of them, and for many of their ancestors, it was often properly conveyed by regarding it as one of a *finny tribe*, or (say) as one of a *scaly breed*. These were the sort of instruments recommended by contemporary handbooks as means of producing elegant poetic utterance. They were not 'mere' synonyms for fish; they evoked quite other and

---

[1] *Inside the Whale* (London, 1940), p. 134.
[2] Cf. *The Critical Review*, vol. 18 (1764), p. 271.

equally important associations;[1] and, for that matter, such circumlocutions may be a good deal more 'informative': *The woodden Guardian of our Privacy/Quick on its Axle turn*,[2] for example, does convey more 'bits' of information than the briefer, and far more usual, *Shut the door*.

We find, then, objectionable or ridiculous in one context uses of words which we already regard as committed to another: 'O Moon', wrote one young housemaid-poetess in what would now be a peculiarly topical, not just a very peculiar, poem.

> O Moon, when I gaze on thy beautiful face,
> Careering along through the boundaries of space,
> The thought has often come into my mind
> If I ever shall see thy glorious behind.[3]

Again, it could have been said in a more acceptably poetic way. I feel sure that Donne could have done it. It is not, then, the 'referent' which amuses us; it is simply that this particular use of the language we are not prepared to call poetry: at least, as poetry, for us (though an audience of housemaids might well have called it 'beautiful'), it is extremely bad. If the poetess had called it parody, we might be prepared to call it good. We do not, for example, regard as good poetry—as it was intended— Leigh Hunt's

> The two divinest things that man has got,
> A lovely woman in a rural spot. . . .[3]

But we do regard as good parody Patmore's

> The two divinest things this world can grab,
> A handsome woman in a hansom cab. . . .[3]

Or, in a context of a very different kind, I personally dislike the use, by British European Airways, of the phrase *passenger-processing*

---

[1] Cf. John Arthos, *The Language of Natural Description in Eighteenth-Century Poetry* (Ann Arbor 1949), pp. 1, 13, 15, 29.

[2] Pope, *Peri Bathous*, ch. 12.

[3] *The Stuffed Owl*, ed. D. B. Wyndham Lewis and Charles Lee (London, 1930, edn. of 1948). Many more examples of this kind may be found in *The Worst English Poets*, ed. Christopher Adams (London, 1958), and among the poems in my own *The Industrial Muse* (London, 1958).

rooms. There is something inhuman about it; and it reminds me of a certain form of cheese. There is also, it seems to me, something rather degrading about the advertisements which advertise *vacancies for female operatives*. But of course, the fault may be entirely my own.

VII

It is, I believe, a narrow and impracticable policy—or, at best, a desperate and superficial remedy—to impose aprioristic verbal panaceas on the complex of experience in even such restricted areas of human activity as those (say) of industry and commerce; still more, on the far, far less restricted area of everyday life. Of course, most of us feel the need for some form of prescriptive-linguistic support; but broad theoretical solutions of our difficulties, principles which are sometimes far removed from the observation of customary and effective practices, are not the most reliable.[1] Nor, as I have said, are many of the short-cuts recommended as methods of arriving at the kind of statement which such principles demand.

And yet, how—if it is unwise to follow these authoritarian prescriptions—can we be sure that the experiences which we wish to convey, will be conveyed? Clearly, it is one, if only one, of the preconditions of success, that we should try to achieve a wide range of expression and a wide catholicity of tastes; not by learning to understand and make use of only certain, and often fragmentary, features of English, but by learning to understand and, so far as possible, make use of the entire potentiality of English. 'Imprecision', as Mr Mittins points out, 'is less likely to derive from failure to operate a chosen construction correctly than from *lack of choice* among constructions.'[2] Of course, trying to master such a highly adaptable medium, trying to make subtle linguistic adjustments the better to communicate subtle experien-

[1] Cf. G. P. Krapp, 'Standards of Speech and their Values', *Modern Philology*, vol. 11 (1913), pp. 57–70.
[2] P. 102 below (my italics).

tial distinctions, 'calls for a more difficult sort of mental activity than' trying to follow precise and invariable prescriptions. But such prescriptions—in so far as they are 'mere figments of the critical imagination'—may 'lead to inhibition of ordered speech and writing, in children whose normal difficulties in expressing themselves' are already 'great enough'.[1] Or they may induce a false and opinionated sense of verbal security, rather than the knowledgeable vigilance which is the price of linguistic precision, in those who consistently subscribe to their use.[2] If grammars or rhetorics are needed, then it seems likely that before one can have a valid prescriptive grammar or rhetoric, one must have a descriptive grammar or rhetoric, which, rather than giving advice about 'what should be said or written, aims at finding out what is said and written', and why it is or is not effective.[3] For it is not by uncritically accepting certain absolute and inflexible 'rules', but by consciously dealing with the actual medium of communication, by familiarizing ourselves with the great diversity of forms and with the great diversity of circumstances in which these forms may be appropriate, that we will come to use (in Jane Austen's phrase) 'the best-chosen language'.

[1] Leonard, *The Doctrine of Correctness*, pp. 244–6. Cf. B. C. Brookes, p. 127 below: 'any attempt to force a particular synthesis inhibits'.

[2] Cf. Noah Webster, *Dissertations* (1789), p. 37: 'They seem not to consider that grammar is formed on language, and not language on grammar. Instead of examining to find what the English language *is*, they endeavor to show what it *ought to be* according to their rules.' (Quoted in C. C. Fries, 'The Rules of Common School Grammars', *Publications of the Modern Language Association of America*, vol. 42 (1927), p. 232.)

[3] O. Jespersen, *Essentials of English Grammar* (London, 1933), p. 19. But cf. Gowers, op. cit., pp. 28 f. As the editors point out in the Introduction above, 'a start has been made on surveying present-day educated English usage in its many forms with a view ultimately to the preparation of realistic and practical teaching-grammars'. Among other attempts being made, in this country, to apply descriptive principles, one might mention the work in progress at the Communication Research Centre of University College London on the language of business and governmental organisations, and the work of Dr P. C. Wason (of the Industrial Psychology Research Group at University College London) on the language of regulations.

Their English, said Harold Urey, the scientist, speaking about American college students in general, 'is very limited. They have little knowledge of grammar and their vocabularies are small'.[1] The situation in this country is very much the same, and I doubt if it will become any better than it is until the importance of English teaching is once more given the recognition it deserves. Of course, one should bear in mind the tragedy of the child from Shou-Ling who was sent to Han-Tan to learn the Han-Tan walk —he failed to master the steps, but spent so much time trying to acquire them that in the end he forgot how one usually walks, and came home to Shou-Ling on all fours. I believe, in fact, that it is only when one can afford to forget the 'idea' of style, that one can, by concentrating attention wholly on the experience to be conveyed, achieve what I should call a 'pure' style—a style in which everything extraneous has been ruthlessly eliminated. But only when one can afford to; for, good as it is to be able to take one's hands off the handlebars, it seems to me unwise to attempt it before one is reasonably well-acquainted, so to speak, with the bike. Take care of the sounds, that is to say, because only then will one be able to devote oneself entirely to the sense— knowing that the sounds will take good care of themselves. I am aware that Tolstoi once said:

> that he had found a passage in a book, which he was writing, very difficult. He hesitated for a long time what to do, but made up his mind and wrote it. Then he decided to test it by means of a game of patience; if the patience came out, that meant that what he had written was good; if it did not come out, then it was bad. The patience did not come out, and Tolstoi said to himself: 'Never mind, it is good as it is!' and he left it as he had written it.[2]

But then, quite apart from anything else, Tolstoi knew his Russian very well.

[1] At the 57th annual convention of the Central Association of Science and Mathematics Teachers in Chicago, 1957.

[2] A. B. Goldenweizer, *Talks with Tolstoi*; quoted in *Writers on Writing*, ed. Walter Allen (London, 1948), p. 229.

CHAPTER 4

Speech education | *J. L. M. Trim*

I

The title of this essay may set some people wondering why the more usual term 'speech training' has not been employed. Upon reflection, they will recall that the letters 'P.T.' have largely disappeared from school curricula and have been replaced by 'P.E.' They will then imagine that I have decided to bring speech work into line with this development and conclude that the word 'training' is no longer respectable in educational circles.

This may well be true. Words are notorious victims of 'guilt by association' and protagonists of a 'child-centred' education may well be averse to using a term commonly associated with soldiers and performing animals.

I have replaced the word 'training' by 'education' because the former seems to imply the imposition of certain mechanical techniques from without, leading to the acquisition of a good voice-production and a good clear pronunciation free from accent and suitable for use on all occasions. Such a training concerns only the most external aspect of spoken language. It is viewed as a useful adjunct to language work proper, but essentially divorced from the deeper, more significant levels of education in the mother tongue, which are better pursued through reading and writing.

It is not my aim to dismiss as useless formal speech work of the type I have outlined. There are, however, grave dangers attendant upon pursuing speech training as an 'absolute' technique isolated from its social context. It may easily lead to inflexibility, a reduction rather than an extension of a person's range of expression, a loss of contact with other people, an increasing immuration of the individual instead of the liberation which education should bring.

It is my contention that it is necessary to take a much wider view and to evolve an approach to speech work from a coherent, developing body of knowledge concerning the nature of spoken language and its role in human affairs. Not only must the teacher work from such a background, but the pupil too should have the sense of a developing linguistic whole, in which special knowledge and special skills are integrated. It is because our spoken language is the matrix of our experience, which it unifies and structures, that I regard the totality of work in spoken language as a humanizing experience deserving the name of an education. My present object is to present some of the evidence in support of this contention.

II

Education begins at birth, and it is to the very earliest months and years that I should first like to draw attention. Undoubtedly the most important educative experience an individual ever undergoes is his first initiation into a language community.[1] This first acquisition of language by a child gives him a place in a community, affords a more intimate *rapport*, a more flexible interaction with other people. It brings him control over much greater forces than his physical strength would allow. Furthermore, it yields the key to ancestral wisdom, for the appropriate use of language embodies the categorization of experience developed over many generations. Once the child grasps the function of words as classifiers, its progress is dramatic. Each actual historical situation is a unique constellation of events—'und in demselben Flusse schwimmst Du nicht zum zweiten Male',

[1] Works dealing with the development of speech and language in children include: M. M. Lewis, *Infant Speech* (London, 1951); O. Jespersen, *Language* (London, 1922); J. Piaget, *Le Langage et la Pensée chez l'Enfant* (Paris, 1923); K. Bühler, *The Mental Development of the Child*, tr. Oscar Oeser (London, 1930.)

said Goethe; we do not swim twice in the same stream. We reduce this chaos to order by identifying recurrent patterns, attaching significance to some features and not to others, noticing some things and ignoring others, establishing significant similarities and differences between events. Language, in its naming aspect, attaches a phonic symbol, simple or complex, to items of this classification. Thus a child, on encountering something new, will say, 'What's that?' in order to see whether the difference it has noticed is embodied in language, and, if it is, to acquire the appropriate label for reinforcement and communication. An encounter with a new word draws attention to some previously unnoticed significant feature of the environment and leads to new experience. 'What's that?' with respect to a word is answered by some practical action or demonstration at first, but increasingly by reference to words previously acquired.

Now, this first critical acquisition of language is carried out through speech. There is no other access to this ordered universe in normal life save through speech. This is the tragedy of the congenitally deaf child. For this reason, the amount and kind of speech stimulation a child receives from its parents is of vital importance. A very great amount of listening is needed before patterns begin to emerge. It is greatly to the advantage of a child who has not yet learned to speak if a great deal of repetitious material is fed to it. That is to say, that while a child is alert, the mother working nearby should verbalize her behaviour and name things as she handles them, not only saying the words in isolation, but placing them in a variety of sentence-frames and using these sentence-frames over and over again with different nouns or verbs as the case may be. Much of this effort will appear at the time to be wasted; the overt behavioural response of the child may well be negligible. We cannot see the brain at work, and the results of its response to this continual stimulation may be apparent only after a considerable lapse of time. It is surprising how many people act as though a baby could understand only what it can itself say. They then provide stimulation only to the level of its active use of language and respond to it by mimicking the sounds it makes. It is not surprising if this stage of its development is unduly prolonged.

It is clear that the speech of the parents acts as a model and as such limits the child's possible attainment. Consequently the kind of speech used by parents to and in the presence of the child is best chosen if it avoids any special baby language, but presents clearly the typical language patterns of the speech community to which the parents belong. These include not only the phonemic patterns—the distinctive oppositions of sound quality upon which all languages are built—but also prosodic patterns such as stress and intonation which apply to sentences as a whole. Persistent crooning removes these means of expression from a child's compass. In short, the development of language in young children through speech is dependent on their stimulation by adults. Those parents whose lives involve a very restricted use of spoken language, taciturn, bookish parents, cooing, crooning, and baby-talking parents, parents in whose speech information-bearing elements are heavily masked, all may well seriously retard the linguistic development of their children.

The active production of speech by very young children is of much less importance. Mastery of the complex sequences of very finely controlled movements necessary for normal speech cannot be expected of them in this field more than in any other. Children vary widely in the skill they achieve and passive language is always more developed than active language. The social pressure towards conformity is rather weak; this is the classically egocentric age and the weight of opinion is that children should not be criticized for poor speech before school age, or treated for it unless there is reason to suspect either some definite organic defect, such as a cleft palate, or, above all, deafness or hardness of hearing. For, in this case, very early diagnosis is imperative. A severely deaf child will, as I have shown, be deprived of the faculty of language itself unless given the most skilled care. There is a special framework of education for the deaf, and, in the field of speech, most valuable and exciting work is being done by teachers of the deaf. Even a partially deaf child will find language difficult and may remain unrecognized; he will be considered of low intelligence and later punished for inattention at school and may well become seriously disturbed. In other cases where active speech development is somewhat retarded, it is usually best for parents to continue to stimulate, act as models and be patient.

By the time school age is reached and formal education begins, the normal child is well integrated into its immediate familiar and local speech community, conforming closely to its norms. If this does not happen, because of some organic or functional defect in the speech mechanism, or some gross developmental retardation, the afflicted child is likely to be penalized by the group as an outsider. In these cases, reference to a qualified speech therapist is to be recommended. But Cockney children who say [fin] for *thin*, or ['i' i'] for *hit it* will not be treated. Whether or not it is desirable for them to speak like this, their use of such forms indicates their success in acquiring the normal speech of their community and in no sense their failure! This strict boundary between the treatment of the abnormal and the education of the normal is often ignored and many self-imposed difficulties result. I wish to deal primarily with the objectives and methods of work in speech education with normal children, who have learnt to move with confidence in their immediate and familiar environment, but have little idea of what lies beyond it.

III

Formal education generally begins with learning to read and write. Speech, from this point on, cannot be equated with language, and though language remains our guide through education and an increased grasp of language one of its principal gains, the question nevertheless arises whether written language alone cannot serve this purpose, whether any specific education in speech is called for at all. I cannot recall having had any myself, apart from learning 'Go Down to Kew in Lilac Time', Wordsworth's 'Daffodils', and one or two other poems by heart.

When it comes to serious work the vast expansion of our experience in and through language is based on its written form. The text-book, admittedly glossed in speech if necessary, and the written exercise, remain the essential tools. Given eyes and hands we can dispense with ears and tongue.

After all, the great expansion of language in science and scholarship has consisted in extending vocabulary, especially the 'open' word-classes: adjectives, verbs, and, above all, nouns. This increased vocabulary can be acquired in writing at least as well as in speech. The written form is easily memorized and various possible pronunciations based on it are usually all recognizable. What one has in notes, or in a book, one has as a permanent possession. A lecture, heard, fades on the air and in the mind, and what remains is not always what is most useful. Furthermore, we learn at school to consider each sentence carefully before we write it down, to ponder alternatives, to eliminate redundancy, to curb an exuberant rush of words to the pen. Now that it is my turn to read students' essays, I appreciate the value of such teaching!

On the other hand, I cannot fail to be aware that this proficiency is purchased at the expense of a full command of spoken language. I have myself a strong tendency to prepare a complete utterance before producing it, so that my contributions to a conversation often consist largely of over-long pauses, with occasional formulated statements which no-one could possibly be expected to grasp at once. Others (-er-) mask these (sort of) pauses by (in a way) using (what might perhaps be termed) verbal pause-equivalents (as it were). This may be done with greater or lesser skill, but it is a skill self-taught, since it has certainly not been considered part of the school's function to teach self-expression through speech in any systematic way.

There is, indeed, little consciousness of any essential difference between spoken and written language, nor any belief that the development of an ability to handle language in speech is of very serious educative value. Our certificates of education involve oral examinations only in foreign languages. Even these have only just become compulsory and are still little more than perfunctory. Speech is considered proper to common life, writing to intellectual and cultural pursuits. The artist in spoken language, even the articulate speaker, is seen as a showy, dangerous fellow, who, like Socrates, will make the weaker case defeat the stronger.

Now this view, that education equals literacy, was perhaps adequate for the age of the three R's, of the railway train and the printing press and the penny post. It is anachronistic in the age of petrol and jet engines, telephones, radio and television, disc- and tape-recording. There can be no doubt that the full effect of these still recent inventions has yet to be felt. I am convinced that we shall all conduct more of our business in speech with a wider range of partners and that writing will find a more restricted place in the ecology of language. Increasingly through speech shall we have to instruct, entertain, and persuade our fellows, and in turn receive instruction and entertainment and decide whether to be persuaded or not.

IV

To appreciate fully why it is that an education based almost exclusively upon written language is unlikely to prepare us adequately to face this new situation, it is necessary to consider more closely the act of linguistic communication itself.[1]

This is a process with a number of distinct stages. A message is formulated and produced by a sender, and transmitted in a particular [medium to a receiver, whose job it is to perceive, recognize and identify, interpret and evaluate it. For example: I think of something I wish to say, fashion it mentally according to the structural possibilities of my variety of the English language, make appropriate movements of my eating and breathing muscles and agitate the air: 'Excuse me, ladies and gentlemen, I am informed that there is a small fire in the building, but there is no immediate danger, so will you please leave calmly but quickly.' The sound waves strike the listeners' ears and they

[1] Cf. Colin Cherry, *On Human Communication* (New York, 1957).

hear the noise. They recognize it as English speech and also recognize some particular speech sounds. They identify the whole utterance as a possible English structure. Relating this to their previous linguistic experience, they bring together meanings of parts of the structure they have met before and construct a meaning for the whole with 'Fire' ringing through their heads.

With written communication, a similar chain of events occurs, except that a different medium is employed, involving different sets of muscles and nerves.

Each act of linguistic communication is thus embedded in an actual concrete situation, and cannot profitably be considered in isolation from it. The situation can be conceived in terms of a number of components: the message itself, externalized in some medium; the sender, the receiver, and the external environment.

To any outside observer, of course, the most accessible components are the message and the environment, but these are far from sufficient in themselves. It is impossible to over-estimate the importance of the background of previous experience, both linguistic and non-linguistic, which the sender and receiver bring to the event. The ease, even the possibility perhaps, of communication between them is dependent upon the congruence of their respective backgrounds. In speech, the early part of any conversation is largely devoted to establishing the degree of congruence, 'placing' the partner, and setting up relations, so that a style of utterance can be chosen which most economically meets the needs of both partners. In a monologue—a lecture, for example—this is not so easily done, though even here the live speaker has a reaction, a 'feed-back' from the listeners, and if he develops a sensitivity, he can adjust his speech accordingly. This sensitivity has to be developed, however, and this again involves study and awareness.

The writer has no immediate 'feed-back' and has to develop a different sense. He must write for a particular envisaged audience and by an act of imaginative projection become that

67

audience and exert a strong selective pressure on his own choice of messages.

The separation of the writer from the reader in time and in space, the fact that their contact is indirect, that there are in fact two distinct situations linked by the written message, does mean, however, that the hand of time lies less heavily upon them. The writer can make notes, write sections as they become clear, uniting them later, ponder difficult problems as long as need be. The reader in turn can read at his own speed, refer back to what he has read earlier, read the last chapter first, skip uninteresting sections and ponder over profound formulations and obscurities. Even in the mechanics of reading we do not follow one line only, but absorb something from adjacent lines at the same time.

In speech, much of this freedom does not exist. The unfolding of the utterance in time is inexorable and speaker and listener alike are bound together in the same situation to the same one-dimensional, one-directional flow of talk. It is essential to effective communication that the activities of speaking and listening (and by this I mean more particularly the hidden events in the mind, formulation on the one hand and identification and evaluation on the other) should be carefully geared to each other. In conversation, this is done by question and answer, and by switching roles. In lecturing, the speaker bears sole responsibility for ensuring that this gearing takes place. For in fact, as an utterance proceeds, speaker and listener are picking their way through a series of choices. There is always a number of ways of continuing an incomplete sentence. The speaker chooses just one of these, and the listener has to identify the choice which has been made, and decide why. At some points, the freedom of choice is considerable, as if I should say, 'Look, there's a . . .' In this case, of course, the probability of any particular word being chosen is low. The information-content of the utterance actually chosen is said to be high. At each point where a choice has to be made a considerable amount of brainwork is demanded of speaker and listener alike, and it is at such points that speech becomes nonfluent.[1] We should therefore be slow to criticize non-fluency. It may just mean that there is more thought going on. More work is demanded of the listener too, since he does not know what to expect and has to identify the less familiar item and then place it in a set of less familiar or less expected contexts. This process takes time, and whereas the speaker pauses before producing part of a critical utterance, the listener can get to work only after-wards, by which time the speaker, having overcome this point, may have a fairly clear passage. Hence the effective pause made by orators after a crucial point, and their keeping key words till the end of a sentence. Hence also, the use of repetitious sentence-frames and 'elegant variation'. Such techniques are prominent in Old Testament poetry, where each half verse often mirrors the other. Sir Winston Churchill's speech in the House of Commons on 4 June 1940, is particularly relevant here! Key sentences ('We shall go on to the end. We shall defend our island whatever the cost may be, we shall never surrender'), themselves synonymous, each prefixed by 'we shall fight them in the . . .', are arranged to form a repetitious framework interspersed with illustrative phrases in an appropriate and climactic order.

The study of these devices of formal rhetoric is of great value in developing effective use of spoken language. There is no danger of creating a nation of rabble-rousers: the English are not so easily roused from their lethargy. In any case, understanding of these devices has a prophylactic value.

This alternation of points of high information with stretches of high redundancy applies also to everyday language. For here, too, when dealing with language units at all levels of com-plexity—phonemes, morphemes, words, phrases, clauses, sen-tences—we find in each case that one choice made restricts or constrains further choices. If one word is known, a better guess can be made at the next. Some types of words are more pre-

[1] Cf. F. Goldmann-Eisler, 'Speech Production and the Predictability of Words in Context', *The Quarterly Journal of Experimental Psychology*, pt. 2, vol. 10 (1958), pp. 96–106, and 'The predictability of words in context and the length of pauses in speech', *Language and Speech*, pt. 3, vol. 1 (1958), pp. 226–31.

dictable than others. Whereas nouns, principal verbs, adjectives, and adverbs are indefinite in number and therefore subject to primarily situational constraints, other word-classes, such as prepositions, articles, and auxiliary verbs, are strictly limited in number, inherently constrained, with a low information-content. All these constraints are cumulative at the phonemic level. Which individual sound unit will occur next becomes more obvious as a word progresses, particularly if the word is long; and of course the shorter the list of words to choose from the more rapidly the listener can identify the word intended. Sequences of highly constrained phonemes require little cerebration in their selection and a minimum in their identification. It is clearly possible for the speaker to present the listener with much less evidence concerning these units than is required at points of decision, and still to achieve successful recognition.

This applies most strongly in formalized situations where the utterance simply stimulates rehearsed actions. A Guards Officer once conducted a complete guard-mounting ceremony with the words 'Onion Sauce'. Any self-respecting R.S.M. or ambitious C.S.M. will ensure that, when he gives a command, *he* can be identified, but not the words of the command. Set religious services are often spoken in the realization that the linguistic units are completely redundant.

It is not possible to balance these ritual utterances by others with no redundancy. The wording of long-distance cables and of papers in technical subjects comes fairly close: such material will, or should, contain a maximum number of words involving choice; but the nearest thing is perhaps the language of mathematics. The vast majority of utterances falls somewhere between the extremes. The conventional phrases with which we accompany routine actions involve little internal choice. H. E. Palmer [1] has pointed out how unexpectedly high a proportion of our everyday language is composed of these fixed, conventional phrases. If the same style of language and speech is used for all purposes, we find either that in familiar situations we are putting a lot of

[1] H. E. Palmer, *Everyday Sentences in Spoken English* (Cambridge, 1922).

work into producing distinctions that are unwanted, or that in intellectual situations the brain cannot cope with the amount of work confronting it, so that a breakdown of communication occurs.

In fact, of course, there is a tendency to equilibrium through the employment of different styles appropriate to different situations. Phonetically, these are characterized by the extent to which contrasts and oppositions are maintained in the chain of speech. Each segment is recognized by virtue of its difference from contiguous segments (contrasts), and from those other segments which could replace it in the same context (oppositions). Thus, *d* in 'they mend kettles' contrasts with *n* and *k*, and is in opposition to the *t* in 'they meant kettles'. The formal style is that in which both contrast and opposition are maximal, giving clarity and distinctness to speech. Redundancy at this level is high. It is appropriate to lighten the load on the listener in some way when his task is made difficult through obscurity of subject matter, noisy conditions, remoteness from the speaker, through being a foreigner or from a different dialect area. Formal style may also be used as a mark of respect or politeness or solemnity. Its use in other contexts is felt to be inappropriate, arising from egocentric considerations on the part of the speaker, and is condemned as pomposity, pretentiousness, priggery, affectation, or pedantry.

The familiar style is that in which contrast and opposition are minimal. In this way, redundancy is reduced. Vowels in unstressed syllables are not only weakened (this is found in formal speech too), but many are elided or omitted altogether. Consonant sequences at word boundaries, which most require rapid movements of a number of speech organs, are simplified, either by eliding a consonant at the end of a word or by replacing it by another more similar in formation to a neighbouring consonant. It is almost invariably the word-final consonant at the point of highest redundancy which is affected. This is why people who attack 'slovenly speech' usually complain that the ends of words are slurred, mumbled, swallowed, or lost. It is also the more frequent alveolar consonants t, d, n, that are primarily affected rather than the less common bilabials p, b, m, and velars k, g. These processes are undoubtedly in accordance with a general developmental tendency of language. Some such process lies between Latin and French—and who now attacks French as slovenly Latin? The resultant language is more compact, much redundancy is eliminated, there are fewer articulatory movements to a given sentence. Sequences are shorter, but at the expense of an increase in the phonemic inventory, so that eventually at least as much maintenance of contrast and opposition is required as before. It is not a lazier, more sluggish, but a more condensed, more exacting language which results. The speaker must organize his utterance faster and more continuously, and the listener has to identify the utterance on the basis of fewer clues, more rapidly presented. His work is much increased.

Of course, this kind of speech is not suitable on every occasion. It presupposes a great deal: a background of considerable common experience, especially linguistic experience, a highly constraining situation, a straightforward relation between speaker and listener—all factors which place the listener in a condition of appropriate expectation. If these factors are strong enough, language itself becomes redundant. Given a man and wife, married ten years, sitting round the fire, and a clock showing 10.15 p.m., ' "mm?" "Hm!" ' is enough to get the man on his feet, fetch two cups of Bournvita (one with sugar and one without) and two welsh-rarebits, put the kettle on for a hot water bottle, put the dog out, and make up the all-night fire. But wherever relations are familiar, the familiar style is appropriate. Indeed the choice of any other style disturbs the intimacy of the relation, being an assertion of other-ness. On the other hand, the use of the familiar style with the wrong people at the wrong time does not remove barriers, it raises them. It is on these occasions that the familiar style is dubbed lazy, slovenly, or careless. In the absence of a close common linguistic background, the listener may simply not understand what is said and a lecturer presenting new ideas to an audience that cannot answer back will leave them far behind in despair if he is niggardly on this level. In fact, straightforward communication situations are not so common as one might think. In general social intercourse we are always concerned to sum up our conversation partners and to make a particular sort of impression on them. An immediate assumption of familiarity and equality is rarely in place: one resents the familiarity of certain salesmen, and, more relevantly in the context of the present discussion, any great degree of familiarity is rarely desirable in the teacher–pupil relationship.

Between the formal and familiar styles there are a number of intermediates—probably in fact a continuum of variation. We have to evaluate the components of a given situation, ascribe some sort of value to it, and match this against some point on the stylistic continuum. People differ somewhat in their assessment of situations and the speech-style they call for, and standards change as the years pass, but there is a good measure of agreement. There is, of course, scope too for individual variation, but if idiosyncracy diverges too far from the norm some breakdown of *rapport* occurs.

Now, most children live their pre-school and out-of-school lives in the family circle and with playmates, and may well employ only the familiar style. This is entirely appropriate. The extension of their range of response in school will therefore be towards the formal. A rather more formal style is perhaps in any case appropriate to the teacher–pupil relation. But there should be no contempt for the speech of the home and of playmates, no imposition of formal speech as a higher, purer, better type, irrespective of context; and, of course, no mangling of speech in the service of spelling.

V

Just as understanding of the causes of stylistic variation can lead to a clearer realization of the objectives we should pursue with regard to 'careful' speech, so a balanced attitude, free from dogmatism, snobbery, or sentimentality, towards the problem of dialectal speech can be achieved through study of the nature of dialectal variation. This problem is best understood by reference to the principle of the arbitrary nature of the linguistic sign discussed by Professor Quirk.[1] This principle is subject to reservations, of course. I should not be happy myself to incorporate it into a definition of language, and it should not be misunderstood as a denial of causality or of the operation of selection pressures in language. It means simply that in no known natural language is there a correlation on any significant scale between the distribution of sounds in root words on the one hand and classes of concepts on the other: the order of words in an alphabetical dictionary has nothing to do with their order in a thesaurus.

We say *tree* rather than *arbre*, *Baum*, *puu*, *dendron*, *djerjevo*, purely and simply because as children we were initiated into an English speech community. To make ourselves understood we have to copy what we hear closely enough for the listener to realize that that is what we are doing. In fact, we copy those about us much more closely than this, so that in general the similarity in the language spoken by different persons varies directly with the extent of their linguistic contact.

The stability of a language community over a period of time will depend on the amount of contact between the three generations generally alive at any one time. A type of society in which a major family unit lives in one house or one small neighbourhood, and great prestige attaches to age, where there is in-breeding and little immigration, will be more conservative than one in which children leave home and district on marriage, allowing their offspring only occasional contact with the grandparents, and more still than one in which children are removed from their parents and communally educated.

The homogeneity of a speech community, geographically, will depend on the extent to which physical communications are developed; on the state of roads, the speed, cheapness, and

[1] Pp. 25 ff. above. Cf. F. de Saussure, *Cours de Linguistique Générale* (Paris, 1949).

efficiency of vehicles, on trade relations, books, postal services, telephone, films, radio and television. In one area at one time variations will be found according to social structure, the number and arrangement of classes and groups, the contact between them, the degree of social mobility or fluidity.

These dimensions give a sort of linguistic space, which it is the task of dialectologists to explore—or would be if they were not too busy hunting linguistic coelocanths. We can place a man within this space, if we know it well—and of course we know the space near ourselves best. The space is not uniformly populated. There are close-knit interlocking clusters, which constitute the dialects of more integrated communities separated by sparsely inhabited spaces. It forms its own little universe. As the forces which hold the universe together weaken, it expands; as they grow stronger, it contracts. That is to say, if a society disintegrates and communications deteriorate—as after the *Völkerwanderungen* or the fall of the Roman Empire, dialects diverge. In a time like ours, as society becomes ever more closely organized, and communications of all sorts are dramatically improved, dialectal differences shrink. This movement correlates highly with age-group dialects. The social and geographical dimensions are also related, since it is the language of the working class, whose lives are the most externally circumscribed, most subject to the pressure of propinquity, that shows the widest geographical variation, whereas the speech of the upper classes, who are educated in a handful of public schools and two universities, who associate and marry on the basis of social, rather than local affinity, who occupy leading positions in all parts of the country, centred on London but constituting 'county' society, is the most homogeneous and the most free from regional association.

We can therefore visualize our dialectal 'universe' as a cone of diminishing volume. Near the base tend to congregate the older working-class folk, who are gradually dying off. The younger an adult is, and the higher in social status, the more likely is his speech to approximate to the 'Received Pronunciation' [RP], which of course represents the apex of the cone. This likelihood is, however, greatest in London, and falls off with the geographical distance from the capital. But it seems to be true of 'Ambridge', too!

The shrinkage of dialects is a much more conscious process than their divergence. People come into contact with many varieties of speech, and may, if they choose, replace their present variety by another, or at least modify it in that direction. One variety is likely to acquire prestige, and become a standard form. This position was reached earlier in written language, as a result of the requirements of printing. Now, the advantages of standardization are so manifest that once established it is unchallenged. Opposition in advance is primarily sentimental, and I personally am not one of those who believe that when the linguist is faced with obscurantist opposition there is nothing he can, or should, do. The colour and variety brought to speech by dialect is external, superficial. We have much more to gain by fully exploiting and enlarging the potentialities of our common speech. When we say, 'I get on well with Smith and Jones, we speak the same language', this is no empty metaphor. The different dialects of English are to some extent different languages. We can communicate fully only within our own group, and some barrier divides us from speakers of a different dialect. Misunderstandings occur, and are all the more insidious because we think we have understood each other. There is a real danger that our sympathy may become limited, our sensibility blunted. To the extent that we find dialect speakers 'quaint' or 'charming', we are less likely to enter into the reality of their problems. It is noteworthy that in drama the role of the dialect speaker has from the earliest times been comic, not tragic. Actors who have had to play serious roles in dialect know how much more difficult it is to engage the full sympathy of an audience. In *Pygmalion*, for example, Eliza comes to life only when she has acquired RP.

In short, convergence towards a standard pronunciation is a natural, progressive response to the conditions of our time. Although those who have done most to codify RP, particularly

Henry Sweet[1] and Daniel Jones,[2] have scrupulously refused to prescribe it as a standard—as befits descriptive scientists—there seems to me no reason to doubt that as the form of speech at the apex of the cone it exerts an attraction and has already become accepted, tacitly, as a standard form of speech. The codification of the phoneticians has caused it to become widely available (it is the form of British English universally taught abroad). Radio and television, moreover, have made its many styles familiar to the entire nation. Its use and propagation in schools are perfectly justified and desirable.

The teacher must, however, be fully aware that accent differences have in the last hundred years been associated with considerable social tensions and individual anxiety. It was about a century ago that the public school system became established with the more or less explicit aim of welding diverse elements into a segregated, self-conscious, homogeneous governing class stamped with a common culture. Habits of pronunciation were immediately recognizable and most difficult to counterfeit, and consequently became the class badge *par excellence*. Although the public schools set out more or less consciously to produce this effect, it is clear that it was in any case a necessary linguistic consequence of a society of 'two nations'.

Had a class structure of this sort become stable and accepted, accents would not of themselves have aroused feelings of hostility. But throughout this period the balance of classes has been changing, and social mobility has been increasing. As a result, class awareness and antagonism sharpened, and differences of accent became a focal issue, characterized by Shaw's famous dictum, 'As soon as an Englishman opens his mouth he makes some other Englishman despise him.'[3] The first working-class children who passed through the new state High Schools were

---

[1] *A Primer of Spoken English*, 4th edn (Oxford, 1932).

[2] *An Outline of English Phonetics*, 8th edn (Cambridge, 1956); *The Pronunciation of English*, 4th edn (Cambridge, 1956); *An English Pronouncing Dictionary*, 11th edn (London, 1956).

[3] Preface to *Pygmalion*.

likely to find themselves between the upper and the nether mill-stones.

The rapid social changes which have occurred in recent years have served to reduce the material inequalities between classes and to increase social mobility to the point where classes are beginning to lose their identity and continuity. As this progresses, and a social structure emerges which commands general accept-ance, the tensions and anxieties associated with accent differences will continue to diminish. The range of difference will decrease, and the residual differences will no longer arouse hostility, envy, or contempt.

These feelings still lie close to the surface, however, and may easily be stirred by tactless handling. For the working-class child, local dialect in a familiar style is the natural speech of home and playmates. To be told by a teacher, with all her prestige and glamour, that this is a disgusting, ugly, slovenly distortion of the beautiful English language, must be traumatic. Such violent, insulting language would force a child to reject the values of either home and playmates or of school. In the sociocentric age between, say, seven and eleven, children are acutely conscious of belonging to a special group, and emphasize its difference from society at large. If school insists on identifying itself with society in opposition to home and gang, the majority will reject it. RP and the world of culture represented by school will be rejected and seen as the badge of a hostile, contemptuous, alien class. The few who make the other choice will become the 'outsiders'. And it is surely not desirable that recruitment for the grammar schools and later the universities, should be primarily from among young people who reject their particular society.

I used to think that the answer lay in 'bilingualism', the use of a familiar style of dialectal speech within the circle of friends and relatives and of a standard language in public life. This is the case, to some extent, in Southern Germany, where the regional accent has no strong social connotations. 'I put on my dialect', a professor at Freiburg University told me, 'when I put on my slippers.'

It will be clear from what I have said earlier that I can no longer regard this as a very likely, or even very desirable solution in England. The maintenance by an individual of two distinct, almost unrelated languages, would correspond to a 'double life', in two distinct societies with no communication between them. In a society which, though fluid, is not, at any rate as yet, homogeneous, it seems probable that most individuals will try to find themselves a place in the continuum of variation which best reconciles their private, professional, and social existences. Of course, a man's speech will still vary to some extent in different contexts, and as in time the range of his contacts changes, the whole range of his speech will be affected. Indeed, if one listens to a comparatively short sample of a person's speech, one can reconstruct much of his biography. The integrity of the personality seems, however, to require that the range of a person's stylistic variation should be continuous and limited to the degree needed to show acceptance of and consideration for the partner.

I think it likely, nevertheless, that as RP becomes increasingly available through mass communication, some approximation to it will become increasingly widespread, and this could prove not only an index of our advance towards a more homogeneous community but also a powerful contribution towards it, and I believe that enlightened teaching, on a wide scale, can play a significant part in this process.

VI

I have dealt with the questions of dialect and 'slovenly speech' at some length, not because they are the most important, but simply because they are a perennial cause of violent public controversy, and are surrounded by misunderstanding. When this is dispersed, a more fruitful field of speech education lies revealed. For speech has dimensions unknown to written language. Written language operates with the choice and arrangement of words. Speech operates not only with these devices but also with features unrecorded in writing, such as tempo, dynamic range, voice quality, and speech melody.

The different kinds of radio commentary provide an interesting study in tempo, or rate of utterance. At one end of the range lies the slow sombre gravity of the solemn royal or religious occasion. Sports commentaries require greater flexibility, as excitement mounts and dies away. Different sports are themselves graded: the occasionally enlivened discursive leisure of a Test Match; the climax of a horse race; the bursts of savage energy in a boxing match; the sustained speed and high-pressure excitement of a Cup Final. Each has its own appropriate tempo, from which alone the sport can be identified given even a small sample.

In addition to changes in tempo, variations in overall loudness and dynamic range can be used to distinguish, say, the principle from the example, or the essential from the marginal. As such it may be used by a lecturer to indicate careful formulation, which should be noted verbatim, as opposed to glosses, which need only be followed and understood. The most effective examples of the use of the device are found in oratory, as in Churchill's speech discussed above, while in the mouth of an unscrupulous judge, the device could be used in a summing-up to combine an impression of impeccable verbal impartiality with a clear directive to a jury.

Voice quality can be varied, amplifying higher harmonics to achieve clarity and audibility at a distance, or suppressing them to achieve a cosy intimacy. There are many other effects which though well appreciated are but little investigated: the icy, the convivial, the edgy, the rasping, the brassy, the reassuring, the soothing. All these are powerful in their effect in the proper context; it is when we allow ourselves to become fixed permanently in one mode, that we lose effectiveness and degenerate into caricatures. Penetrating audibility in a public speaker is one thing: in a woman companion it is quite another. And, as for the icy voice, it repels unwelcome strangers and welcome visitors alike.

Chief among these means of expression specific to speech is

intonation, compound of rhythm and melodic patterns. It is still not generally realized that in English we have a regular, ordered, closely structured system of intonation patterns which we apply to the various sentence structures to get fine distinctions of meaning. They are hinted at in punctuation, but are otherwise unrecorded in normal orthography. Let me illustrate briefly the effect of some patterns by attaching them to the sentence, *It's not bad*:

It's not bad ·‾\ (a plain statement)

It's not bad ·‾\ (enthusiastic)

It's not bad ·‾/ (reassuring)

It's not bad ·__/ (surly)

It's not bad ·‾/ (querying: *Do you mean to say that* ...)

It's not bad ·\∨ (hesitant, insinuating that it is not very good)

That's not a style I've ever worn, pronounced as in the first of the above examples, is final, and will send a salesman off looking for another dress. But *That's not a style I've ever worn*, uttered with the intonation pattern of the last example, sounds uncertain, and no self-respecting salesman would stop short of a sale. Like the other direct phonic means of communication, intonation is not available for use in written language and instead we have recourse to lexical and syntactical devices. I have heard a 'linguistic philosopher' complain that English has no explicit means of conveying distinctions of attitude because it does not employ special words for the purpose, and dismiss 'tone of voice' as primitive, clumsy, and inexact. In fact, intonation patterns are ideally suited to convey such distinctions, which cannot readily be fitted into a number of discrete categories. The fact that we find it difficult to formulate the meaning of a given intonation simply shows that words cannot do the same job, not that intonation is imprecise. Admittedly, a large proportion of misunderstandings and intuitive dislikes, both individual and international, are due to an incongruence, incompatibility, failure to communicate, on this level. The principal reason is our ignorance of the intonation systems of other dialects and other languages, which we have not yet learned to translate. Within the same speech community, however, while a certain number of speakers do deviate widely in their use and evaluation of intonation patterns, and a very few are quite insensitive to them, there is close agreement on the force of these intonations among most speakers.

In recent years many phoneticians have devoted close attention to this fascinating and rewarding study. As a result, the main features of English intonation have now been codified, and a suitable notation evolved.[1] Some modern grammars of English [2] are incorporating descriptions of intonation, though as yet the treatment is generally confined to an appendix or special section. The stage has been reached where no English specialist can regard himself as fully competent if he lacks a thorough understanding and command of this fundamental resource of the English language.

VII

How then, in the light of the above considerations, should schools best undertake the teaching of spoken English? An increasing number of authorities are recognizing its importance by appointing specialist teachers of speech and drama. In such

[1] For example, R. Kingdon, *The Groundwork of English Intonation* (London, 1958); M. Schubiger, *English Intonation* (Tübingen, 1958); L. E. Armstrong and I. C. Ward, *A Handbook of English Intonation*, 2nd edn (Cambridge, 1950); W. Jassem, *Intonation of Conversational English* (Wrocław, 1952).

[2] For example, Adolf Lamprecht, *Grammatik der Englischen Sprache* (Berlin, 1958).

cases the work of the specialist will occupy a focal position. Nevertheless, the bulk of such appointments are part-time, and even a full-time specialist cannot expect to enjoy more than a limited contact with any particular class. It is most important that schools should create an atmosphere, a favourable environment within which a child's speech can develop. In this task all teachers have a part to play. Their speech is presented continuously to the pupils and exercises a powerful formative influence for good or ill. The child growing up in a school where the speech of the teaching staff is a homogeneous and well-modulated colloquial RP will be at a great advantage. Furthermore, every teacher of English should be informed with knowledge and understanding of both the mother-dialect of the pupils and of the national or regional language of culture being made available to them. Speech education should then concentrate initially upon developing power of expression within the child's native speech. Later, drama can be used to place the child in fresh situations which call for new style, types, and usages of language, gradually expanding in range and observed in finer detail.

Eventually an atmosphere of acceptance will be created, based upon an understanding of the part played in our language by formal speech and a non-regional standard pronunciation. Then and then only should formal speech training be undertaken. Language work of a formal nature, in speech as in grammar, has recently been under a cloud. Pursued without understanding as an end in itself, isolated from and indeed in conscious opposition to the child's natural language, formal training may indeed be arid. The reaction may, however, go too far. Some educationists, basing themselves upon ideas deriving ultimately from the mystique surrounding Gestalt psychology, hold that man is an organism greater than the sum of its parts, that language is one integrated aspect of a global pattern of activity which can be influenced only in its totality. Just as dissection kills the organism it investigates, so that the secret of its life is lost, so, they claim, analysis yields only a dead anatomy, while the true essence escapes.

As is often the case, the positive aspects of this argument are valid and fruitful, while the negative assertions are suspect and restrictive. Provided that formal speech training, based upon analysis, is conducted within the framework of a wider conception of language, and in the consciousness that it is not self-sufficient, let alone an end in itself, it is by no means inimical to the general development of personality, and affords the most efficient and economic method of teaching a given pronunciation.

The nature and extent of formal teaching to be undertaken will vary of course with the ability and co-operation of the class. I would suggest, however, that the phonetic method widely used in foreign language teaching is capable of wide application to the mother tongue, both in building up awareness of the nature and resources of the type of English spoken by the children, in comparing this with other types of English, and, if desirable, teaching these. A phonetic notation showing speech-sounds, stress, and intonation is the basic tool. Given a phonetic notation, it becomes possible to discuss the differences between careful and familiar speech intelligibly, making sense of both.[1] It becomes possible to point out in objective terms the differences between a dialectal and a standard pronunciation, as one would treat differences in the sound-systems of distinct languages. This again is more likely to gain acceptance than comparisons in terms of value-judgements. Ability to observe speech accurately can be greatly improved by the dictation of passages of English of different types and in different styles, while actual aural discrimination can be trained by dictation of meaningless sound sequences. Both types should of course be taken down in a phonetic notation. Dictations can be given by members of the class as well as by the teacher, which increases the sense of participation. Finally, the problem of acquiring different types of pronunciation becomes a challenge to individual skill. Children love producing bizarre noises, but are usually discouraged from doing so. If, however, we regard them as accomplishments, we

[1] Cf. J. D. O'Connor, *New Phonetic Readings from Modern English Literature* (Berne, 1948).

84

may be better able to guide this oral experimentation, until the pupil can produce at will a wide variety of sounds, intonations, voice qualities, and know what he is doing. In this respect, tape-recordings are useful to accustom pupils to the sound of their own voices.

I have of course not invented these methods. They have been the basis of practical work in the Phonetics Departments at University College London and elsewhere for many years and have been applied to the study of foreign languages, particularly to English as a foreign language, with considerable success. Teachers who have applied them to speech training problems have also found them successful. In one case, a colleague reported to me that he had employed them 'as a last resort' with an unco-operative group of fourteen-year-old London grammar school boys, and found that their attitude had changed to one of en-thusiastic co-operation within a few weeks. That they have not been tried more widely, that they are in fact comparatively unknown, is indeed one further sad illustration of the lack of communication between the different groups of workers in the field of speech.

Perhaps the greatest advantage of these methods, which I have no more than cursorily outlined, is that they develop inner resources, and do not require the constant presence of a teacher or model. It becomes possible, for example, to leave the question of which type or style of speech to use and in what contexts, to the judgement of the individual, in the light of his understanding of the workings of spoken language. Different individuals will undoubtedly arrive at different solutions, and may well revise their decisions as time goes on. We are unlikely to be in a position to judge the full effect of such an education in spoken language until some years after a pupil has left school.

I shall summarize my conclusions. It is not in isolation, but as an integrated component of education in language, that speech education is to be pursued: not in terms of some ready-made technique of voice production, nor in terms of a standard pro-nunciation in a formal style; not, at any rate, in terms of these alone, as ends in themselves; much less in terms of corrections of 'errors' and 'vulgarisms', irresponsible denunciations, intemperate in language and deficient in logic, with which the correspondence columns of journals and newspapers have made us sadly familiar. Our aim in all language work is not to root out heresy and error, to impose standards; it is to liberate the individual from the limitations of his immediate environment, to enable him to expand the range of situations that he can experience and manipulate without loss of identity and with increasing self-awareness. Success in using language lies in matching distinct situations with appropriately distinct utterances, and our language has more than enough resources for this purpose. Failure, arising from ignorance or disregard of these resources, lies in rigidity and poverty of response. None of us can of course expect to command the whole resources of a language: a language is, as it were, a country greater than any of its speakers may encompass. We can hope at best to find our way over its main roads and perhaps explore some small areas more closely on foot. There will be one place probably where we feel most at home, but if we stay there and despise the rest of the world, we shall be dull fellows indeed.

CHAPTER **5**

The teaching of English in
schools | *W. H. Mittins*

I

My subject clearly needs narrowing down to manageable proportions. I am persuaded by a combination of factors—including the framework of this symposium, the nature of my own teaching experience, and my views on which aspects of the teaching of English most need attention today—to concentrate rather on secondary than on primary school work, and more on linguistic than on literary matters, in so far as these can be separated.

We ought, however, to take a quick look at the whole field first. If we do this through the eyes of A. N. Whitehead, we may at the same time get a possible clue to why the English course is perhaps more satisfactory at the earlier stages than later. Whitehead, it will be remembered, sets up a theory—an interesting and to my mind persuasive theory—of a 'rhythm of education'. He distinguishes three broad stages of mental growth —stages of romance, precision, and generalization. These divisions are of course only rough; there are overlaps and there are, as it were, sub-cycles within the main cycle. The timing of the stages is also rough. It varies, moreover, in different areas of study; for instance, the whole cycle starts later in the sciences than in language.

In the area of language, the transition from the stage of romance to the stage of precision corresponds more or less with the transfer from primary to secondary schooling. In Whitehead's own words:

D

As he nears the end of the great romance the cyclic course of growth is swinging the child over towards an aptitude for exact knowledge. Language is now the natural subject-matter for concentrated attack. . . . Accordingly, from the age of eleven onwards there is wanted a gradually increasing concentration towards precise knowledge of language. Finally, the three years from 12 to 15 should be dominated by a mass attack upon language, so planned that a definite result, in itself worth having, is thereby achieved. . . .

Towards the age of fifteen the age of precision in language and of romance in science draws to its close, to be succeeded by a period of generalisation in language and of precision in science. . . . In this stage the precise study of grammar and composition is discontinued, and the language study is confined to reading the literature with emphasised attention to its ideas and to the general history in which it is embedded.[1]

To what extent is this rhythmical progression evident in English studies in school? I would suggest that the approximation is often close in the primary years; that there is some approximation again—though of a more superficial kind—at the end of the school course; but that in between, in the main years of secondary schooling, there is comparatively little correspondence.

The stage of romance is commonly recognizable in primary school practice. Increasingly, in infant and junior classes, the acquisition of the new skills of writing and reading has the quality of adventure, of discovery, of 'first apprehension'. Language is presented as a means of extending power over experience; and large and exciting fields of new experience are opened up through stories, plays, and poetry. Novelty is exploited and curiosity encouraged. Boundaries between subjects, between lessons, between work and play do not generally exercise much restraining influence—at least, not until late in the junior school, when the eleven-plus examination, with its objective tests and one-word answers, may be allowed to impose a degree of cramping formality. If my impressions are accurate and representative —and I realize that I am indulging in very broad generalizations —then, in the sense of relevance to the needs of children, work at this early stage of 'romance' is essentially, if somewhat paradoxically, realistic.

[1] *The Aims of Education and Other Essays* (London, 1932, edn of 1950), pp. 35–9.

The common pattern of English studies at the other end of the school course, especially at the point of transition to sixth-form work in the grammar and technical school, has also some affinity with Whitehead's 'rhythm of education'. The 'study of grammar and composition' (whether it has been precise or not) 'is discontinued, and the language study is confined to reading the literature'. This change of emphasis, however, would seem to derive less from considerations of psychological relevance such as operate in the primary school than from the structure of the General Certificate of Education examination; language as a separate examination subject ceases at Ordinary Level. The correspondence between current practice and Whitehead's 'stage of generalisation' seems, in fact, almost adventitious. It is implicit, both in Whitehead's theory and in G.C.E. regulations, that by about the age of sixteen the language has been more or less mastered and is available for the exploration of ideas in general. But in practice it is seen that this assumption of mastery cannot safely be made. That is probably one reason for the increasing popularity at sixth-form level of 'general' papers and for the increasing emphasis in literature papers on the comprehension and criticism of 'unseen' passages. There is, in fact, a growing awareness that the study of language as such needs to be pursued beyond Ordinary Level. The samples of actual writing by adolescents and adults which I shall be quoting seem to support this contention.

That the virtual cessation of specific language study after Ordinary Level appears to be premature does not necessarily undermine Whitehead's theory. Given in the main secondary school years that 'gradually increasing concentration towards precise knowledge of language' and that 'mass attack upon language' which he stipulates as appropriate to this 'age of precision', then the assumption of a reasonable mastery of language by the age of sixteen might be more nearly justified. But, as I see it, the average secondary-school English course does not readily invoke the notions of 'concentration', 'mass attack', and 'precision'. Too often it is a thing of shreds and patches. To some extent this is in the nature of things. Language, in its function as a medium for the expression and communication of the most variegated and disparate experiences, is subject to strong centrifugal tendencies. In consequence the English syllabus not only tends to fragment into the conventional compartments of language and literature, with sub-divisions for composition, grammar, and vocabulary, and for poetry, prose, and drama, but also spills over from both of these spheres in very diverse directions—into current affairs, play-acting, debating, journalism, logic, choral speaking, italic handwriting, miming, puppetry, and a host of other no doubt excellent but diffuse activities.

It is this multifarious character that provokes the familiar reproach that English studies lack discipline. And, however admirable the separate activities may be in themselves, they cannot be conducive to concentration in the pursuit of precision unless they are geared to a central purpose. I believe that uncertainty about central purpose, about the dominant aims and objectives of the English curriculum, is a major cause of that lack of precision in the use of language which rightly causes great concern at many different levels of our society.

It would be wrong not to substantiate my criticism by quoting some evidence. Before doing this, however, it is only fair to concede that standards in English usage are by no means determined solely by teachers of English, who have much less of a monopoly of their 'subject' than have most of their colleagues. It is probably even more true today than it was in 1918, when the Board of Education published one of its manuals for the guidance of teachers, that 'within the school itself, it is not entirely, nor indeed mainly, in the "English" lessons that English is being taught and learned'.[1] Most pupils start school with facility of a kind in the oral skills of speaking and listening. The teacher of English initiates the further processes of reading and writing. But thereafter he is but one agency in the business of linguistic development. Of the many other agencies (his colleagues, the

[1] *Suggestions for the Consideration of Teachers in Public Elementary Schools* (London, 1918), p. 23.

children's families and friends, the 'mass media' of newspapers, films, radio, television, comics, and the like) not all are allies. In truth the most powerful—press, cinema, broadcasting—are in many ways positively hostile to healthy language growth, in so far as they discourage critical attitudes to experience and to discourse.

A curious repercussion of the sort of competition a teacher of English may have to meet from popular commercial stereotypes came my way recently, in the form of a G.C.E. Ordinary Level composition. The writer is describing how presence of mind once saved her from disaster:

While I was dancing, and the band was playing the hot tango rhythms the Italians love so well, I had seen him watching me. His small, shifty dark eyes had gazed at me hungrily, scanning my body, my face, and my dress. I knew then that he desired me with all the passion that the Italians possess. They are a hot-blooded race. . . .

The writer is pursued and caught by the amorous Italian:

His huge hands began to stroke my hair, my face, and my arms. He was whispering to me in Italian. I could not understand him and I did not desire his kisses or his false love-making. . . . What was he going to do? Where was he taking me?

I was shivering both from cold and fear. My eyes must have been huge and veiled with mystification as I stared up at him. . . .

She fights for her virtue. Frustrated, he tries to strangle her. But at this point the narrative rather disappointingly resorts to a familiar school formula. An alarm-clock awakens her in the nick of time:

The thick leather-backed novel which I had been reading before I had gone to sleep, looked up at me. The title on the cover was the answer to my terrifying nightmare. It was 'The Horrors of Naples at Night'.

Between the lines of this, with its technical competence of phrasing, one can sense the struggle in a lively mind between genuine literacy and the sub-cultural values of 'admass'. In the clash of this struggle the still small voice of the teacher of English is scarcely heard.

Another adverse factor, reducing the English teacher's effectiveness of control over his subject, is the growing complexity of modern life, with its accelerating rate of change. Language inevitably tends to lag behind and to be inadequate to the new demands experience makes upon it. This inadequacy takes various forms. An obvious and simple example at adult level is lexical inadequacy in scientific contexts. A year or two ago, for instance, a writer in *Nature* pointed out how aviation experts, having invented a remarkably intricate piece of engineering, of the class of aerodynes but neither aeroplane nor helicopter, could not find a suitable word for it. In the end they resorted to the amusing but technically feeble label of *flying bedstead*.[1]

Lexical weakness of this kind is unavoidable in a world like ours; in any case it is the least serious deficiency of its kind, operating, as it does, mainly in very specialist fields and at an advanced level. Far more serious and widespread is inadequacy in syntax. This occurs very frequently, in school and after school, at all levels of society and in all kinds of situation. Perhaps I may be permitted to illustrate it by quoting some samples, taken from a fairly wide range of writing. I am aware of some of the pitfalls in the collecting of linguistic monstrosities, in particular of the danger of special pleading through unrepresentative sampling. I can only say that I have chosen my examples from a very large number, leaving unused many that are worse as well as some that are better as specimens of English usage.

II

Since the detection of error and weakness in language is an occupational disease of teachers and examiners of English, let me start with a quotation from another subject, geography. It is one of a number collected under the significant title 'Some O-Level Horrors' in an article in an educational journal.[2] The compiler used it to illustrate 'the extreme poverty in English

[1] Vol. 176 (31 December 1955), p. 1250.
[2] *Times Educational Supplement* (15 November 1957).

which hampers very many G.C.E. candidates'. It purports to describe a piece of scenery shown in a photograph:

The region is hot and rainless because of the nature of the sandhills. There is no vegetation, because of the absence of rain. There are frequent sandstorms because of the shape of the sandhills. The sun is hot because of the clothes of the men.

The inadequacy here is perhaps not as unpardonable as the examiner seems to think. Its weakness derives almost entirely from the writer's inability to appreciate the difference—the fairly subtle difference—between '*x* causes *y*' (that is, lack of rain causes lack of vegetation) and '*x* leads me to infer *y*' (not 'the sun is hot because of the clothes of the men', but 'I infer from the clothes of the men that the sun is hot'). Nevertheless it is seriously inadequate. The writer could not, in the somewhat trying circumstances in which he was writing, call readily upon the range of syntactical structures needed to match the range of his ideas.

This lack of versatility in sentence-structure seems to me to be a root cause of the poverty-stricken, threadbare quality of much contemporary writing (not to mention speech). None of us dare claim immunity. I do not think, for instance, that the youngster just quoted need fear comparison with the distinguished professor of psychology whose article in a reputable scientific journal contains the remarkable sentence:

Some dogs form conditioned reflexes quickly and strongly, and can only be extinguished with difficulty; other dogs form conditioned reflexes slowly and weakly, and can be extinguished with extreme rapidity.

Lest I seem to ally myself with those who, on this issue, make a scapegoat of the scientist and his jargon, I hasten to cap this example with a much more outrageous specimen from a well-known authority on English usage. It occurs in a booklet aptly entitled *English Gone Wrong*, but not as a quotation under fire. It is, sad to say, a part of the text:

The six terms I have extricated from the congeries of potentials are to be regarded as forming one of those enclaves of congruity, set in a raging wilderness of disparates, which I am attempting to establish, not only, though mainly,

93

for the convenience of the valiant reader but also for the assistance of the luckless author.[1]

Here, not only is the vocabulary insufferably pretentious, but the sentence-structure is on the verge of collapse.

Let me return to the school end of the scale by quoting from a sixth-form essay:

With the aid of weather stations in many parts of the world manned by highly skilled scientists, who collect data on weather conditions around their particular area, this is done with the aid of many instruments.

Again the weakness is basically structural. The writer embarks upon the construction of a fairly elaborate periodic or 'suspended' sentence, but is unable to retain his grasp of the pattern through a succession of subordinate statements. He is lost by the time the main clause is due. Accordingly he slips in a desperate comma and adds a completely fresh sentence.

Any or all of these lapses may, of course, be quite unrepresentative of their perpetrators and as such excusable. One is less ready to find excuses for similar failures in the English of potential teachers, for whom scrupulousness in the use of language is a most important professional qualification. When, as not infrequently happens, graduate students in our departments of education seem incapable of coping in words with the notions they seek to express, we sometimes try to convince ourselves that the failure arises from the novelty of educational studies for them. They could, we tentatively suggest, speak and write satisfactorily about anything else. There is probably something in this argument, but it can hardly apply to the graduate in social science who, writing in her own time on a topic chosen by her as falling within her specialist field, produced the sentence:

As it is a social unit on its own, the school will present certain problems within itself, but the school can also help, or not help, any child confronted, not caused entirely, or necessarily at all, by the school.

This gelatinous, pulpy sort of English is more than an occasional phenomenon; each year's essays, dissertations and, of

[1] E. Partridge, *English Gone Wrong* (London, 1957), p. 29.

course, examinations raise a fair crop. Scientists and Fine Art students tend to produce rather more than their share, but Arts graduates do not lag far behind. Even an honours degree in English is no guarantee against gross mismanagement of the language. It was, for example, a second-class honours English graduate who, making a very simple point in a routine essay, wrote:

Often subjects overlap [in a Modern School] more than in a grammar school since there staff tends to refrain from dealing in too much detail with someone else's subject—in a good geography lesson history plays its part: French Canadians in Canada: in a lesson the teacher may be drawn into a discussion of why they are there and how Wolfe took Quebec; handicraft and gardening will involve mathematics.

This reminds me of one of Gerald Kersh's 'men without bones', in the gruesome story of that title. 'It was not unlike a human being', we are told. 'It had eyes, and there were vestiges—or rudiments—of head, and neck, and a kind of limb.' But in the heat of the sun it melted into a 'glutinous grey puddle'.

Even vestigial traces of structure can disappear in the examination room. There the unnatural tension may lead to further degeneration, as in this quotation from another English honours graduate, ironically enough discussing alleged illiteracy in G.C.E. work:

The writer might indeed be a result of the poor level of attainment he is criticising [sic] as he does not take care to use his words accurate.

It would be easy but too depressing to extend this lamentable catalogue of failures in writing. It would be more difficult to demonstrate similar shortcomings in speaking, listening, and reading—but only because these other skills leave no tangible deposit that can be readily reproduced. No one who uses public transport or listens to popular broadcasts can be very optimistic about standards of speech. And many teachers—not only of English—would endorse today Professor I. A. Richards' assertion over twenty years ago that 'every candid teacher knows already . . . that . . . the majority of his pupils at the end of all their schooling understand remarkably little of what they hear or read'.[1]

III

But let me turn to more constructive considerations. However widely one spreads the blame for the unsatisfactory state of affairs I have been illustrating, the main responsibility for doing something about it admittedly rests on the shoulders of the teacher of English. What then can he do to help the individual pupil to 'take care to use his words accurate'? The prime need, as I have already suggested, is for a regrouping of forces into a more coherent, tightly organized programme. Some teachers, concerned about those centrifugal tendencies I have mentioned, seek to achieve a kind of concentration and continuity by methodically working through batteries of vocabulary exercises in slot-filling, finding synonyms and antonyms, substituting words for phrases and the like, through progressive tests in précis-writing, through a course in comprehension, through a closely circumscribed system of clause analysis, and sometimes even through the formal dissection of set books with full note-taking apparatus. I do not think this approach gets to the heart of the problem, whatever its incidental value (and from a good teacher much may be learnt in spite of his methods). It tends to achieve its systematic character at the cost of constantly directing attention to preselected utterances which are often and inevitably detached from the experience of the pupil. In consequence it runs a serious risk of degenerating into what has been called 'mere verbalism'.

The position of the teacher of English in relation to the problem of 'verbalism' is peculiarly difficult. While attacking the unthinking misuse of language, he must avoid discouraging an experimental and adventurous attitude to words. He must temper but not utterly extinguish that infatuation with words which is a common feature of adolescence. By the age of fifteen to sixteen the stage of uncritical exuberance should have yielded in some

[1] *Interpretation in Teaching* (London, 1938), p. (v).

degree to the discipline of clear thinking and exact expression. As an extreme example of the kind of verbal intoxication which has escaped this discipline, I would like to quote from another G.C.E. Ordinary Level composition. The writer is supposed to be giving an account of a rescue. Under the startling title of 'The Bitter Cantabrians', he (or dare I suggest that it is more probably she?) describes how 'the torpid soil stretched down to the sparkling waters of a shimmering lagoon. . . .'

In the pulchritude of this sylvan scene a bleached villa stood silhouetted against the monotonous sweep of the horizon.

One day as Phoebus's chariot brought pencils of lambent flame streaming through my shutters, igniting every mote of dust in its wake, I rose, and walked out on to my balcony, which was scented by the aromatic perfume of sun-kissed vines. . . .

Hearing 'the acoustics of faint shouts' up in the mountains, the narrator goes to the rescue of a gypsy stranded on a mountain ledge. They get down just before nightfall:

Then all at once the bleeding sky merged into an ebony obscurity and Diana's waning citron cosmos lay cradled in fleecy clouds in the east.

It would be foolish, of course, to hold any teacher, or any method of teaching, responsible for this sort of thing. I quote it merely as a sensational example of the 'word-spinning' that may occur in less dramatic form and, on a smaller scale, in a good deal of so-called vocabulary work.

Returning from this excursion into 'verbalism' to my main argument, I would suggest that text-book lessons with numbered short exercises, however systematic they may on the surface seem to be, cannot supply that central unifying force which English studies often lack. We therefore want a better alternative. This, I contend, is to be found in what Professor Quirk urges in the second of these papers, when he stresses the need 'to re-invigorate or re-introduce English language teaching in the schools and training colleges'.[1] This, if I understand it correctly, means what Whitehead meant by 'the precise study of grammar and

[1] P. 10 above.

97

composition' and by 'a mass attack upon language, so planned that a definite result, in itself worth having, is thereby achieved'.

I have as yet deliberately avoided focusing on the term 'grammar', so varied and vexatious are its connotations and so controversial its status in the English syllabus. In so doing I have been conscious of I. A. Richards' horrid warning:

The word ['grammar'] has been pronounced, its influence descends upon the scene, and with it a strange and deadly cramp seems to spread over the intellectual faculties, afflicting them with squint, making them unable to observe all sorts of things they are perfectly conversant with in normal life.[1]

I hasten to remove one source of possible confusion by saying that I am not calling for the rehabilitation of that kind of traditional formal quasi-Latin grammar which I was brought up on and which is still taught, though often only half-heartedly, in some English and most Scottish schools. The content of what I shall call the 'old' grammar is by no means entirely useless for our purposes, but the underlying principles have been long since shown by linguists to be in many respects unsound. As Professor C. C. Fries puts it, 'the conventional "formal grammar" is, like the Ptolemaic astronomy, falsely oriented'.[2]

Scholars in the United States and in this country, unlike some who have sought to dismiss the old grammar from the classroom, are trying to replace it with a new grammar based on more reliable principles. They have in particular done much to disentangle the confusions of formal and logical categories which bedevil the older grammars. Progress in implementing their findings in the classroom has been faster in America than here. James Sledd was actually reviewing some school grammars when he wrote not long ago:

For a long time, a good many American linguists and teachers of English have been urging that the English grammar taught in our schools should be made linguistically respectable. They have found it easy to show the absurdity of much that is now taught, but until recently they have not provided the better text-books which are necessary to the success of their argument.[3]

[1] *Interpretation in Teaching*, p. 183.

[2] *The Structure of English* (New York, 1952), p. 277.

[3] *Language*, vol. 33 (1957), p. 261.

We need in this country text-books similar to those referred to, similar for instance to Dr Paul Roberts' *Patterns of English*[1]— though not, one hopes, so big and expensive. Such grammars could provide English with a coherent linguistic discipline. The central position that a reformed grammar might occupy is perhaps confirmed by the tendency of the essays in this volume to converge on the grammatical sector. Structural linguistics— which Professor Quirk has discussed—offers a set of categories the distribution of which in connected discourse is of the essence of style. 'Matters of style', Mr Warburg reminds us, 'are necessarily linguistic matters.'[2] Furthermore, since the new grammar insists on the priority of speech patterns and involves the examination of phonological structures (using the concepts of phonemes, intonation, stress, pitch, and juncture) it has important common ground with speech education, which is discussed by Mr Trim above.

This broader, more inclusive conception of grammar bridges two of the widest gaps which have opened up in English teaching —the gap between grammar and style and that between speech and writing. Both distinctions are useful, but neither is absolute. In regard to the former, for instance, we may agree with Professor Simeon Potter that 'It is important to distinguish *grammatical necessity*, which implies that the speaker has no choice of form if he consents to follow accepted usage, from *stylistic possibility*, which allows him to choose between two or more given constructions'.[3] At the same time we may argue that at a more fundamental level grammar and style merge indistinguishably; we may endorse R. C. Pooley's contention that 'the building of sentences and the manipulation of sentence materials for improved style are at the very centre of grammar instruction and are the chief reason for the teaching of grammar'.[4]

The inclusion of some phonology—sometimes linked with the

---

[1] *Patterns of English* (New York, 1956).
[2] P. 39 above.
[3] *Modern Linguistics* (London, 1957), p. 108.
[4] *Teaching English Grammar* (New York, 1957), p. 107.

more familiar grammatical material through punctuation—is one of the distinctive features of the new grammar books. Another, and a more fundamental, one is the emphasis on basic sentence patterns. In place of the conventional but unscientifically discriminated eight or nine parts of speech, we are given form classes, structure groups, word clusters, and test frames, differentiated, not in terms of meaning, but in terms of structure, word-order, and arrangement. The new grammar seems in fact to offer a set of accurate observations about how language really works, such as the old grammar fails to provide. Whatever one's eventual views on its validity and its usefulness for school teaching, it deserves in its own right close examination by every teacher of English.

It is not possible here and now to go into detail about content; in any case, even in the United States, the long and difficult process of sifting and adapting for school use the evidence provided by linguists has only just begun. There are awkward decisions to be taken on policy—on, for example, the degree of simplification and compromise permissible. Should we, for instance, continue to use the traditional terminology, though with fresh connotations? Or should we cut our losses and invest in a new nomenclature, after the manner of Professor Fries's Class 1, Class 2, etc. words?

In so far as one can detect broad lines of development, it would seem safe to forecast that, if the traditional parts of speech terminology is kept at all and if definition of some sort is thought desirable, then the mode of definition is likely to be strictly functional. James A. Walker, in an unpublished report quoted by Pooley,[1] lists a set of such definitions. A noun, he suggests, is 'a word that behaves in a sentence like the word *blackness*'. Similarly a verb is a word that behaves like *blacken*, an adjective behaves like *blackish*, and an adverb behaves like *blackishly*. For each of these four 'form classes' he adds the reminder that 'no word is a noun/verb, etc. outside of a sentence and in and of itself'.

Recognition of the parts of speech so discriminated is clearly

[1] Op. cit., p. 109.

an empirical matter. The student finds experimentally the 'test frame' into which any item fits and identifies it accordingly. The repertory of possible test frames constitutes a set of basic sentence patterns. These simple sentences are variations on a mere handful of arrangements of subjects, verbs, objects, and complements. Single words are in all cases replaceable by functionally equivalent clusters. Compound and complex sentences are elaborations where one or more of the clusters is itself a predication. Questions and other non-declarative formulations are distinguished by variations in word-order or intonation or both.

The emphasis on function and pattern makes it possible to dispense not only with much of the traditional apparatus of rules and definitions but also with the business of sub-classification of parts of speech, paradigms, parsing, and other complexities that derive from a preoccupation with the separable word rather than with the sentence. In consequence, there can be a considerable economy in categories and terminology.

IV

In my own view, the new grammar is markedly superior to the old on practical as well as on theoretical grounds. It can be a weapon against that poverty of language which—much more than misspelling, mispunctuation, wrongly-chosen words, technical lapses in grammatical concord, and other easily isolated errors—is the most disturbing feature of modern English usage. It serves a higher purpose than correctness—namely, resourcefulness. The traditional insistence on correctness can impoverish expression rather than improve it. Just as the child may learn to avoid the penalty of spelling corrections by choosing simpler or more familiar words like *get*, *nice*, or *big* where *receive*, *agreeable*, or *colossal* would be more appropriate but tactically less advisable, so too he may avoid committing himself to more complex sentence-structure if the grammar he is studying seems to him 'an elaborate arrangement of booby-traps'. The new grammar differs by being descriptive rather than prescriptive; it offers to the student, not rules and embargoes, but a repertoire of the structural resources of his language. Through it, especially if his linguistic studies are reinforced by sensitive and meaningful contact with the rich verbal patterns of expert literature, he may well stand his best chance of developing that 'feel for' appropriateness in language which is the key to all effective communication.

I do not think there is any inconsistency in my emphasizing both precision and resourcefulness. On the contrary, precision in language depends more on resourcefulness than on grammatical correctness. Imprecision is less likely to derive from failure to operate a chosen construction correctly than from lack of choice among constructions. To be precise one needs the ability to select from a number of possible formulations that arrangement of the appropriate words best suited to the meaning which the utterance is designed to serve. The samples of poor English I have quoted demonstrate, I think, that this ability cannot be assumed to arrive by a natural process of growth. Lack of the ability accounts for a large proportion of defects of construction—dangling participles, ambiguous qualifications, Fowler's 'unequal bedfellows or defective double harness', and many others. In school it leads to statements like:

To realise the trouble changing a tyre in dense fog has to be done to be believed.

Or, by a potential emigrant to Canada:

The occupation that I would like to do would become a Farmer in the area of Fort William where the main occupation is that of wheat growing. But the only trouble there is that in winter when the ground is covered with snow there is no work for the Farm hands because what cattle the farmer has he can feed them hiself so that the other men have to go into the Towns and Cities to find work.

At present one can only speculate as to whether a reformed kind of language teaching would have much corrective influence on writing like this. It is not likely to do so if it proves as intractable for children as the old grammar. Of that R. B. McKerrow once justly remarked that it 'was not really intelligible to students until they had already passed beyond the stage of mastery of the language at which it might conceivably have been of use to them'.[1] Research like that of W. J. Macauley[2] in Scotland has shown that recognition of the parts of speech as presented seriatim in the old formal grammar is beyond the capacity of any but the brighter and older children. Other research, especially in America, has shown that this same approach has little or no bearing on the avoidance of error in composition. But these findings may well mean no more than that there is little purpose in teaching an unsatisfactory kind of grammar. There seems reason to hope that a grammar based on current linguistic theory, with its greater accuracy, consistency, and realism, would prove both simpler and more fruitful. Certainly, I suggest, it deserves a trial.

To be fair, such a trial would involve systematic and regular language teaching; I doubt whether any grammar can properly be taught incidentally, as is sometimes recommended, though of course cross-references to grammatical points may well be made in the course of other kinds of lesson. The most promising method of teaching in the language study lesson proper is, I think, inductive and empirical in approach, working—as far as is consistent with orderly progress—from samples of real utterances to patterns and principles, rather than the other way round. These samples might come from the pupils' own speech and writing, from their reading of literature, and also from such public sources as notice-boards, shop-windows, advertisements, the radio and newspapers. To take one example: newspaper headlines, as has often been remarked, especially since the results of H. Straumann's investigation were published in 1935,[3] often make excellent starting-points for linguistic discussion. The frequent omission from a headline of those essential signals (such as determiners or articles) that distinguish its structure from other

[1] 'English Grammar and Grammars', *Essays and Studies of the English Association*, vol. 8 (1922), p. 148.

[2] 'The Difficulty of Grammar', *British Journal of Educational Psychology*, vol. 18 (November 1947).

[3] *Newspaper Headlines: A Study of Linguistic Method* (London, 1935).

structures focuses attention—in stimulating, practical, and often amusing fashion—upon important problems of syntax. Lively and profitable language lessons, even with comparatively weak students, may develop from the examination of specimens like *HEALTH SERVICE BAN STAYS*, *BURY SMALLPOX SUSPECTS*, or *GIANT WAVES DOWN QUEEN MARY'S FUNNEL*. The interest generated by such an approach might even help to overcome that language-resistance—the Americans call it 'logophobia'—which some teachers claim to be meeting more and more.

The ambiguity which characterizes many headlines and other public announcements (*PRIVATE CAR PARK*, for instance) is after all in a sense complementary to resourcefulness, as Professor Richards points out in his latest book:

It is better, more politic and wiser, not to call this versatility of words by any such evil-sounding name as 'ambiguity'. Let us call it 'resourcefulness' instead.[1]

I would like to see experiments in language courses using this approach, not only in grammar schools, but also with the verbally less sophisticated children in Modern Schools, though the pace and content would naturally be moderated for them.

V

To any objection that sufficient time is not available I would answer that room should be made by displacing other kinds of lesson. The most dispensable routine in English work in schools is —as I have already hinted—that devoted to batteries of very short exercises alleged to refine and extend vocabulary, to promote conciseness of phrasing, to improve punctuation or to eliminate grammatical error. Watching English teaching in schools of all sorts leads me reluctantly to believe that anything up to a third of the time allocated to 'English' may be spent on these text-book procedures—and often to very little teaching, as distinct from testing, purpose. Most experienced teachers are

[1] *Speculative Instruments* (London, 1955), p. 75.

doubtless more selective and critical in the use of these exercises than the students in training whom I see in action. I certainly hope they are better informed; for even the honours English graduate can add a surprising element of unreliability to proceedings ostensibly objective—as, for example, the one who was recently dealing with the sentence: *I will not speak to a pupil who reads what I write with so little care.* She very properly accepted the moving of *with so little care* in accordance with the principle of proximity, but also demanded inverted commas round *what I write* (viz. *I will not speak to a pupil who reads with so little care 'what I write'*). The next sentence, *When at sea in a vessel the horizon is always circular,* defeated both teacher and class, who could find nothing wrong with it.

It would, however, be over-optimistic to assume that the standard of teaching in this kind of lesson, even in the hands of a practised teacher, is considerably higher than the standard of the text-book used. And the latter standard, in the majority of the books of exercises that proliferate in our schools, seems to me to fall at times regrettably low. My objection is primarily, not to the high incidence of odd specimens of English (for example, *Cinders had fallen in a circle from Fleet Street to Newgate Market*), but to the basic fallacy that discrimination between words and usages can usefully be developed in the insufficient contexts provided by single sentences. The multiplicity of items in the ordinary run of these text-books clearly but unjustifiably implies that it is possible to make snap decisions about the suitability or correctness of one word or phrase rather than another on the evidence of a single sentence. For instance—and as before I draw my illustrations only from lessons I have attended while preparing this paper—why should a class which has clearly never heard of Dr Spooner be asked to agree that many amusing *anecdotes* (rather than *stories*, *fables*, or *legends*) are related to that gentleman? Or that we were met at the lonely inn with *cold comfort*—not *cool*, *icy*, *frigid*, or *chilly comfort*? Why should they curtail the sentence *These services were free, gratis, and for nothing*? In the first of these sentences there is no value in choosing the word *anecdote* unless one appreciates both its overlap with the other terms and its special differentiating characteristics—and this cannot be done without much fuller contexts for all the terms. In the second sentence—the *cold comfort* one—as in many of these exercises, success means the establishment or reinforcement of a cliché. In the third a facetious formula, *free, gratis, and for nothing*, which is rarely if ever used except in a jocular setting where it is entirely suitable, is stigmatized as tautologous because in other settings it would be unsuitable.

If exercises like these—and one could quote many more, involving the insertion of punctuation marks, the elimination of the verb *get* (in these we do not *get up* in the mornings—we *arise*), and so on—are handled in the manner and at a fraction of the pace implied by the form and size of the text-books, they are indeed the merest verbalism or shadow-boxing. If, on the other hand, they are used critically—that is, if they are 'contextualized' (to use Professor J. R. Firth's term[1])—then they serve a purpose which could be much more effectively served by starting from contexts provided by children's reading and other experiences.

It has often been pointed out that the use of formal exercises to develop vocabulary and allied skills is unsound psychologically. Dr A. F. Watts, for example, assured us many years ago that:

The enrichment and illumination of experience by observation and discussion is a surer way to the genuine enlargement of vocabulary than can be secured by concentration on formal exercises in the correct use of words the need for which is not personally felt.[2]

Linguistically the practice is no easier to defend than psychologically. It ignores or at least blurs the fact that meaning is subtle, fluctuating, and elusive. R. G. Collingwood has a picturesque figure for this:

The proper meaning of a word . . . is never something upon which the bird sits perched like a gull on a stone; it is something over which the word hovers like

---

[1] 'The Technique of Semantics', in his *Papers in Linguistics 1934-51* (London, 1957), p. 10.

[2] *The Language and Mental Development of Children* (London, 1944), p. 58.

a gull over a ship's stern. Trying to fix the proper meaning in our minds is like coaxing the gull to settle in the rigging.[1]

Colin Cherry uses a homelier figure:

Words do not carry 'meanings' tied around their necks, like labels round pots of jam.[2]

One would like, I suggest, to see in English lessons less label-tying and more gull-coaxing.

This point of view agrees with Whitehead's contention that 'there is not a sentence which adequately states its own meaning'.[3] It reminds us that sizeable language units must be provided if meaningful discourse rather than mere word-manipulation is to take place. This requirement is met in some degree by the familiar kind of comprehension work, at least by contrast with batteries of shorter exercises, though of course not to the exclusion of the even larger units of full-scale composition and literature. The case for comprehension exercises has been investigated very thoroughly by the London Association for the Teaching of English. The Association's Secretary of Studies, Mr Britton, has recently reported on correlations obtained between comprehension tests on the one hand and intelligence, vocabulary, and composition tests on the other. He notes that, rather surprisingly at first glance, it is the composition test (not the intelligence or vocabulary test) that contributes most to the overlap between the two sides, even though it differs from all the others in requiring initiation of language instead of response to it. Looking for a common element to account for this overlap, he finds it in the fact that both comprehension and composition are concerned with continuous language, whereas all the others deal in 'bits and pieces of language'.

Time might therefore well be saved for better things by economizing in work on 'bits and pieces of language'. Another—and a related—economy, urged long enough by authorities such

[1] *The Principles of Art* (Oxford, 1938), p. 7.
[2] '"Communication Theory"—and Human Behaviour', in *Studies in Communication* (London, 1955), p. 67.
[3] *Essays in Science and Philosophy* (London, 1948), p. 73.

as Sir Philip Hartog and Professor Gurrey, would be a drastic reduction in the time spent on routine class corrections. But I have not space to elaborate on this point.

Nor have I left myself space to do more than glance at the literature lesson as such. My concentration on the language end of the spectrum of English studies has been deliberate, because I feel that it is there that repairs are most urgently required. But I would stress that language and literature are parts of the same spectrum. English is one subject, not two, whatever the examination and time-table arrangements may suggest. The difference between language and literature lessons is a difference of angle and tactics. Whereas in the language lesson the emphasis is commonly on initiation rather than response, on practice and instruction rather than experience, literature is primarily a matter of enjoyment. But enjoyment is inseparable from understanding, discrimination, and—at a due stage of maturity—criticism. Stylistics, properly understood, occupies an intermediate position on the spectrum. It offers common ground for creative composition by the young writer on the one hand and critical analysis of the work of the established writer on the other. As Professor Quirk puts it, 'the teaching of language needs literature among its prime material' and 'literature is best studied when the study of language is to hand as an ancillary'.[1]

A more or less complete merging of the two areas is appropriate to senior secondary school pupils, but at earlier stages the interaction will naturally be less explicit. There the main objective is to encourage the appreciation rather than the analysis of literature. This appreciation will include, one hopes, intuitive response to the patterns of language employed, and this response will be made increasingly explicit as the capacity for criticism emerges. But there is an obvious danger of rushing the process, of making premature demands for evaluation and analysis. Robert Frost's well-known comment that 'Poetry begins in delight and ends in wisdom' is applicable to literature in general, and teachers forgo or shorten the stage of delight at their peril.

[1] P. 8 above.

My impression is that in fact teachers are more willing today than they used to be to accept enjoyment, not only as the first objective of literature lessons, but also as in the long run conducive to the growth of skill in language. They are increasingly willing to accept the truism that literature cannot be taught in the usual sense of the term 'teach'. Their problem is largely the highly individual one of finding a personal style of *not* teaching it —of letting it teach itself. There has, I think, been real progress in this direction. There are far more lessons *in* literature and far fewer *about* literature. Nevertheless the importance of the teacher's not coming between writer and reader cannot be exaggerated. One therefore welcomes such reminders as that given a year or two ago by a committee of teachers in a stimulating report on the teaching of poetry. There it is firmly stated, perhaps slightly overstated, that 'D. H. Lawrence's "Snake" needs for introduction no map of Sicily, no knowledge of snakes, no facts about Lawrence. It is self-sufficient.'[1]

I would conclude by expressing the hope that my criticisms do not seem unjustly harsh, and my firm belief that the job of teaching English today is not only of the greatest importance, but also of the greatest difficulty. It is so difficult, in fact, that one wonders, not that the results are sometimes disappointing, but that one is not disappointed more often.

[1] Central Committee on Teaching of English in East and West Ridings of Yorkshire, *Poetry and Children* (London, 1956), p. 7.

CHAPTER 6

The teaching of English to scientists and engineers | *B. C. Brookes*

I

'Once upon a time', wrote Cecil Day Lewis, 'poetry and science were one, and its name was Magic.'[1] Yet today most of my engineering students would agree with Sam Weller that 'Poetry's unnat'ral; no man ever talked poetry 'cept a beadle on boxin' day . . .'. They might even agree with the poet Cowper that 'talking is necessary in a tête à tête to distinguish the persons of the drama from the chairs they sit on'. To see how this divergence has come about, and thus to understand some of our present difficulties in teaching English to scientists and engineers we must first glance at some history, at the condition of scientific literature today, and at the relation between language and communication. Finally, I shall briefly describe the course I have evolved for electrical engineers at University College London.

In England there has been an intellectual coolness between men of letters and men of science since modern science was founded in the seventeenth century. At that time, Latin was regarded in all countries of Western Europe as the only possible medium of academic communication. The languages of Shakespeare, of Montaigne, and of Dante were still regarded as fit only for the imprecisions of everyday life, for the ephemera of practical affairs and the scribblings of popular writers. Latin alone had power to support eternal truth. But the great innovators of the seventeenth century, Galileo and Descartes among them but with Newton as an exception, symbolized their conflict with the

[1] *The Poet's Way of Knowledge* (Cambridge, 1957), p. 3.

Establishment by writing even their major works in the vernacular. The first scientific societies founded in the cultural centres of Western Europe also adopted the vernacular for their discourse. In London the founders of the Royal Society went still further. They rejected the 'amplifications, digressions and swellings of style' that characterized the literature of their day; they exacted from their colleagues 'a close, natural, naked way of speaking' and preferred 'the language of artisans, countrymen and merchants before that of wits and scholars'.[1] They had slammed the door against their literary and classical colleagues.

But the Royal Society soon lost its zeal for simplicity of diction. Though the front door had been slammed the back door was left wide open. By the end of the eighteenth century scientists were beginning to specialize; the Linnean Society had been founded and the Geological and Astronomical Societies were soon to follow. And these specialists began to raid the rich stores of the classical lexicons to name the new discriminations they were creating. There was no longer a single scientific dialect that could be distinguished from the language of letters, but a number of distinguishable dialects, each characterized by a growing family of contrived technical terms borrowed from Latin and Greek.

During the next phase, that of increasing specialization, there was no *rapprochement* between the men of letters and the men of science in England. But on the Continent the history of scientific literature was somewhat different. In France, Descartes had early established a standard of logic and clarity, but, during the eighteenth century, science was adopted—not wholly to its advantage—as a subject fit for literature. Voltaire asked why 'the study of physics should crush the flowers of poetry. Is truth so wretched that it cannot endure ornament?' And so the presentation of science became an exercise in fine writing. Here is a fraction of a sentence from Buffon's thirty-six-volume *Histoire Naturelle* (1749–88) which, in my English translation, cannot of

[1] Sir Henry G. Lyons, *The Royal Society 1660–1940* (Cambridge, 1944), p. 54. The quotations are from Thomas Spratt, the first historian of the Royal Society.

course match the grandeur of the original: 'The noblest conquest that man has ever made is that of the proud and spirited animal which shares with him the fatigues of war and the glories of battle; as dauntless as his master, it sees peril and confronts it; growing accustomed to the clash of arms, it delights in it, seeking it out and joining the fray; it also seeks man's pleasures, at the hunt, at the tournament, on the turf, where it shines and sparkles; but, as docile as it is courageous, it does not allow itself to be carried away. . . .' And neither must I. Buffon, of course, is referring to *Equus caballus*, the domestic horse. It is magnificent, but it is not science. 'Le style, c'est l'homme même', says Buffon, and his style reveals the *littérateur*, not the scientist.

Though scientists may repudiate Buffon's claim to the name of scientist, nevertheless Buffon and others, notably the popularizer Fontenelle, achieved for science in France something that has not yet been achieved for science in England. They made science respectable to the literary élite. And an important result of this achievement is that the French scientist has always had a regard for his language and a pride in his writing that English scientists only rarely acquire. Here is a French professor of mycology concluding a treatise on the language of science, in 1946, and quoting with approval the comment on the French language, 'Si ce n'est pas le langage des dieux, c'est celui de la raison et de la vérité.' [1]

In Germany, too, science found the support of men of letters. The organization of science in Germany was handicapped by the diffusion of scientific activity among its many provincial capitals and by academic reluctance to recognize in German a language fit to be heard in a German university. But the dominant figure in German literature, the great Goethe himself, wrote treatises on optics and morphology, and considered them to be his greatest works. Again, though his scientific work is not now highly regarded, Goethe demonstrated to Germans that science was not unworthy of the respect and attention of the humanist. His reward is the respect with which German scientists regard their language and their literature.

[1] E. J. Gilbert, *Langage de la Science* (Paris, 1945), p. 301.

In England, the scientific writer has never had such support; in fact he has been almost wholly ignored. Where he has not been ignored, he has been damned by the faintest of faint praise. George Saintsbury writes of Darwin's style: 'It is very clear; it is not in the least slovenly and there is about it the indefinable sense that the writer might have been a much greater writer, simply as such, than he is if he had cared to take the trouble and he had not been almost solely intent upon his matter.'[1] Lascelles Abercrombie says that *The Origin of Species* can be regarded as literature 'if we ignore Darwin's purpose and simply regard for its own sake the expression he designed to serve his purpose'.[2] Ford Madox Ford writes: 'Records of facts, statistics and scientific theories are always so swiftly superseded that in a very few years almost no trace of them remains on the public consciousness. We may doubt, for instance, if any people today read Darwin's *Origin of Species*—a word which, some decades ago, shook the civilised world.'[3] Middleton Murry says that 'a proposition in Euclid is an elementary example of good style, though in an absolutely non-creative kind'.[4]

These quotations represent a common but injudicious attitude to scientific literature. The scientist must always be intent upon his matter and his purpose, and must wonder how they can be separated from their expression. Moreover, the scientist expects his theories to be shortly superseded; if he hopes for lasting fame it is not in the expectation that his theory will become a dogma, but only that his part in the great inquiry will be remembered. To say of the writing in which geometry was founded that it is 'absolutely non-creative' means to the scientist that the critic must be using these words in a highly technical sense peculiar to literary criticism. And of all the scientific writings that the critics might have chosen as demonstrations that 'they left no

[1] *A History of Nineteenth Century Literature* (London, 1896), p. 301.

[2] 'Principles of Literary Criticism', in *An Outline of Modern Knowledge*, ed. William Rose (London, 1932), p. 868.

[3] *The March of Literature* (London, 1938), p. 16.

[4] *The Problem of Style* (Oxford, 1922, edn of 1949), p. 58.

trace on the public consciousness', it is odd that they should have selected *The Origin of Species*—except that it seems to be the only modern scientific book that is generally known to literary critics. The men of letters seem still to hear echoes of the scientists' slamming of the door in their faces three hundred years ago.

In general, the attitude of these English critics to scientific writing permeates the English departments of our schools and universities. Literature and science are wholly separated; there is at best a coolness between them. It does not surprise me, therefore, to find that most of the science and engineering students I have met in recent years have shown towards literature and writing an attitude that is usually resentful, sometimes hostile, often contemptuous. They refuse to accept that literature has any relevance for them either as scientists or as human beings. But we cannot blame the students; they are brought into the quarrel at an early age.

It seems to me that little can be done to make the teaching of English more effective for scientists until school teachers of English and literary critics begin to take a warmer interest in the characteristics which differentiate scientific from literary writing, and to study the problems of communication which are peculiar to the scientist. In the best scientific writing they will find not only such qualities as precision and imagination, which the man of letters might claim as his own, but also directness, balance, intellectual honesty, objectivity, and humility, qualities which are not so common that they should go unrecognized. A defect of our education of scientists and engineers is that they are not normally made acquainted with models of the best scientific writing, nor are its essential qualities made known to them. Young scientists are given no acceptable ideal to strive towards in their writing; they are left to work out their own solution to their literary problems, and all too few realize that they have a problem at all. I hope, therefore, that teachers of English will try to introduce some good popular science books into their syllabuses of reading. A list of seven hundred books on popular science approved by the British Association has been published quite recently.[1]

Above all, the English teacher must remember that contempt breeds contempt. A single slighting reference by him to science or its literature, any echo of the comments of the critics I have quoted, can, in the presence of pupils already committed to science, undo years of his own patient work. No new technique of teaching is worth trying until confidence between the English teacher and his pupils is fully established; his respect for their science will win their respect for his literature.

II

I turn now to the present condition of scientific writing. We must recognize the necessity of documents to science; without documents there would be no science. The lay public and the young science student may picture the scientist as wholly busy with his machines and instruments—with his 'hardware' and 'plumbing'. Certainly, the glimpses the public is offered of scientific activity by press or television or other means, seem to focus on the more material manifestations of science. But these are usually the end, or the means to an end, of an activity that has depended on documents of many kinds—on notes, reports, diagrams, and calculations—composed in the dialects that scientists and engineers use in their discourse. The public is not shown these documents. Even the scientist himself often forgets their importance to him.

Whatever else science may be it is not simply a great heap of facts. It is above all a public social activity which wholly depends on communication between its practioners. Any scientist who claims to have made a discovery, must, before his claim can be conceded, report his findings in the appropriate dialect to scientific colleagues able to criticize his report and to assess its scientific significance. It does not suffice to run through the streets joyfully crying 'Eureka! Eureka!' A report or paper must be

[1] The National Book League, *Science for All* (Cambridge, 1957).

written. Anyone engaged in scientific work who is incapable of making this kind of report is not a scientist but a technician, not an engineer but a mechanic. The scientist or technologist demonstrates his expertise, as does any other intellectual, by discoursing with his fellows in their technical dialect; proficiency in his written and spoken dialect is a badge which cannot be counterfeit. The technician, on the other hand, demonstrates his expertise, as does any other craftsman, by manipulating physical structures and materials with the particular skill he commands; he could be illiterate and yet be a highly skilled mechanic.

To discover something new in science is an achievement of which the discoverer can be justly proud; it is not unworthy of him, if the needs of national security or of commercial prudence permit, to hope that he will be publicly credited with the advance he has made. But as almost every research activity is likely to be duplicated elsewhere, and as an increasingly intensive spirit of international competition pervades our society, there is increasing pressure on the research scientist to claim his priority of discovery as quickly as possible. In this country the usual procedure is for the scientist to describe the gist of his claim in a letter to the editors of *Nature* with a promise to report his work more fully 'elsewhere'. Though this pressure to claim priority has happily reduced the reluctance of the scientist to put his pen to paper, the risk of losing priority in the present frenzy of research activity in some fields may lead to hasty and ill-considered reports.

The most marked characteristic of scientific literature today is not its originality, however, but its bulk. There is far too much of it. The last edition of the *World List of Scientific Periodicals* listed forty-six thousand titles. No scientist could both attend as he should to his research and read all that he should about work related to his own without using the services of the abstractors and the reviews of recent advances. But these abstracts and summaries, essential though they are, add yet more to the pile of paper. And the pile is inflated by duplication: the same work may be presented by the same author in the different forms appropriate to several different journals, by the reporting of trivialities (since the competence of a research scientist is sometimes measured by his output of papers), and by a large amount of paper circulated for administrative rather than for communicative purposes. By 'communicative purposes' here, I mean 'intended to be read', by 'administrative purposes' I mean 'intended only to be seen'—as evidence of activity. Too much of the paper that is circulated in the name of science is written to satisfy administrators that the research departments for which he may be responsible are in fact operating; a document written in an unintelligible dialect is convincing evidence that the research man is earning his salary. But all this paper, important and unimportant, somehow gets mixed up together and the resulting problem of selection for a research department (now called 'literature retrieval') is one which perhaps only a computer will completely solve. The problem would be less formidable if we could return to the more civilized tempo and attitude of the nineteenth century and our scientists could adopt, as Gauss did, the motto: *Pauca sed matura*. Certainly no external restraint, no censorship, can be imposed.

Not everything a scientist writes will appear in the form in which he wrote it. Between him and the publication of his paper there lurk, shadowy and secretive, the referees who have to assess the fitness of his paper for the journal to which it is submitted. And then, after rewriting and rearranging and reducing his paper by half to meet the referee's criticisms, once again it is intercepted on its way to publication, this time by the technical editor of the journal. His task is to pummel the paper into conformity with the 'house style' of his journal. At last, the paper, battered into submission, may find peace in a quiet corner of the journal, labelled with its exhausted author's name and college.

This submitting of science papers to ordeal by referee and editor has, of course, the legitimate purpose of maintaining a high standard of publication. But even referees and editors are human and therefore sometimes err. If a person is asked to criticize something, he feels bound to utter some criticism, if only to demonstrate that he has paid attention to it and earned his fee.

Anyone can verify my observations by circulating a paper among his colleagues and asking them to criticize it in turn. If after meeting each criticism the paper is retyped and passed to the next colleague in turn one will probably find, I predict, that nothing is permanent but change. Even the same critic, after a decent interval, can be shown to contradict himself. There is no absolute of perfection in presenting a science paper but only a number of versions that are, as far as anyone can see, about as good as each other. Literary criticism, even of scientific papers, is not an exact science; subjective value-judgements have to be made. The editor, a practical man, avoids the risk of interminable dispute by appealing to authority—his own authority. The editor's decision is final—it has to be. But the teacher of English is not an editor: his criticism of his pupils' work should never suggest to them that he has an inner vision of perfection that they can never hope to attain.

Whatever his teacher does, the young scientific author soon learns after leaving school that there is no perfection in writing. He learns that however carefully he prepares any paper for publication it is possible that it will be returned to him with the request for drastic revision. His natural reaction to this kind of treatment is to spend less care in preparing his next paper. That will certainly need some editing. So the editor finds more work to do and, brandishing the offending manuscript, loudly complains about the illiteracy of scientists. He therefore feels justified in appointing more editorial staff who in turn do more editing. So, finally, the young scientist, unable to see the point of the criticisms made of his papers, contents himself by submitting his first rough draft and returning to his bench and to the work he can understand. The vicious circle is complete. American publishers of science books now appoint teams of technical editors to shape the rough-hewn manuscripts submitted to them.

I have exaggerated, of course. But it has to be realized that the more that scientific writing is edited, the less the scientist feels his personal responsibility for what is published in his name, and the less care he will give to his writing.

In industry, the position is even worse. Technical editors and technical writers, all loudly complaining of the illiteracy of their scientist colleagues, increasingly intervene between the scientist and those for whom he writes. They write the scientist's papers for him, perhaps from rough notes or even from discussions with him. In part, their activities may be justified; they are experts in knowing what different kinds of readers are looking for, and they can save time which a research man can more profitably use. But, in so far as they relieve the scientist of his responsibility for writing a coherent record of his work for his scientist colleagues, they are relieving him of his first duty as a scientist and helping to reduce a research man to an inarticulate technician. In the long run, this is not good for science. There is no way of revealing the weaknesses in a research programme, of stimulating alternative approaches, of indicating possible developments, as effective as writing an account of the work. But the writing must be done by the scientist concerned and not by an amanuensis.

It is for the English teacher to correct the distorted picture of scientific research that is presented to the public and which is often misleadingly attractive to the schoolboy who dislikes writing; research is not wholly a game played with exciting toys; the hard work of writing is an essential part of it and, though perhaps only in the long run, the quality of a man's research is measured by the quality of his writing about it.

III

Now I must consider the scientist in industry who is not doing research but who is applying his scientific or engineering knowledge to practical ends. Occasionally I am asked to advise industrial organizations about the reports their applied scientists and engineers are writing. The samples sent for my inspection usually demonstrate clearly that something is wrong. Grammatical and syntactical faults abound. A superficial examination would lead the critic to conclude that a short revision course in English grammar and some remarks on style appropriate to their apparent needs would meet the situation. It does not. It is not possible to teach English grammar directly to a group of scientists, even though some of them may make private inquiries about specific points. They feel that grammar is largely irrelevant to their needs—I have often found them to be right—and above all they cannot stomach its illogical and pretentious technical jargon. If I pay an exploratory visit to the works or department concerned and have informal discussions with the men themselves, I almost always find that the root cause of the poor reports is not ignorance of English grammar (though they may indeed be ignorant of grammar), not uncertainty about the structure and logical development of reports or papers (though there may be differences of opinion), but either inadequate facilities or uncertainty of purpose.

I find that writing is hard work even in the quiet of my study. The writing of a paper of several thousand words means assembling the material that may be needed, making a selection from it to meet the specific requirements of the paper, ordering the material in a logical sequence, interpreting the material for the intended reader after assessing what he already knows of the subject, and presenting it in a coherent, balanced, and readable form. Yet often I find that the men whose reports are complained of are expected to undertake this complex activity, which demands some mental detachment from the world at large, perhaps in the din of a factory, perhaps in a less noisy office, but with constant interruption by telephones or colleagues. It is remarkable, not that their papers are written badly, but that they are written well enough for mistakes to be discernible and therefore to be corrected. Scientific authors in their predicament can often be rescued from the taint of illiteracy simply by persuading their managers to provide a sanctuary, a library, or a writing room without a telephone, in which an hour or two of un-interrupted quietness can be guaranteed for them.

The writing of reports and papers is hard mental work even when one knows what one is doing. It is harder still if one has no clear purpose or end in view. A piece of practical writing such as a report is an instrument which can be judged to be 'good' or 'bad' only in so far as it meets or fails to meet some specified practical purpose. The only valid criterion for assessing the value of a report is the comparison of what it does with what it was intended to do. The scientist and engineer usually appreciate this point; the man of letters, as we have seen from the criticisms I have quoted, sometimes applies different criteria. An engineer, for example, never designs an instrument or machine *per se*; he always has a detailed specification to work to. The machine he is asked to design, let us say an electric motor, must be planned to use a specified power supply and to convert that power into a specified mechanical performance of torque or speed or acceleration and so on. Only when such data are available can he begin his detailed design. The same kind of specification is needed for all practical writing. Why is the report needed? What has it to do? For whom is it intended? What knowledge of the subject can the intended readers be presumed to have already? The more detailed the specification the easier it is to write the report and the more likely it is that those who called for it will get what they want.

It is my experience that much of the bad writing complained of in industry arises simply because the authors are uncertain of the purpose of their assignment. A scientist who is uncertain of his purpose or of his subject will reflect his uncertainty in grammatical and syntactical faults, will betray his aimlessness in sudden switches of points of view, and his hesitancy and indecision in the unbalanced and illogical structure of his paper. But a scientist who has something to say and a clear purpose in saying it is usually able to write his paper in a clear plain style that is, with one serious reservation, adequate for the occasion. The reservation I have to make is that I often find scientific writing cluttered up with woolly phrases and tired words— words which 'have so much play in their gears that they no longer click', to use a phrase of Brice Parain's [1]—words such as 'problem', 'factor', or 'development'. Such words and phrases are

---

[1] *Recherches sur la Nature et les Fonctions du Langage* (Paris, 1942), p. 145.

liable to grow over the sentence-structure of scientific writing like barnacles over a ship's bottom; clear them away and the stream-lined structure emerges from the shapeless mass. Any faults become apparent and can be at once repaired.

The lesson here for the English teacher concerned with science pupils is, I suggest, to ask them sometimes to write about scientific topics which interest them, and to explain to him—someone they know—aspects of their work. For his part, the teacher should be ready to acknowledge his ignorance of science—if ignorant he be—and should demand explanations and descriptions that are adequate to his own understanding. Such a task provides the science pupil not only with an exercise in English composition, but also, if the teacher plays the game with honesty and sincerity, with a real exercise in communication. Writing to such a specification, narrow though it may seem, still leaves the pupil-author with scope for his imagination in invent-ing illuminating analogies. And the teacher's theme should be: 'If your paper is not plain and logical to me, then it is not good *science*.'

Though scientists are always ready to learn some new labora-tory technique, they are less ready to admit that writing too is a skill that must be learned. What Sir Joshua Reynolds said of the painter is equally true of the scientist: 'A provision of endless apparatus, a bustle of infinite enquiry is employed to evade and shuffle off real labour—the real labour of thinking.' More directly, Agnes Arber writing of the botanist says that 'the mechanical pleasure of cutting endless microtome sections may lull the mind into serene inaction and comfortable passivity in regard to the problem to be solved'.[1] But writing always demands mental effort. The least demand upon his writing skill is made when the scientist, able to give full rein to his specialist dialect, writes about his research for other specialists. A heavier demand is made on his skill when he writes about his work for laymen; he has to restrain his use of dialect and try to imagine how his own conceptual world looks to a man who cannot know it.

[1] *The Mind and the Eye* (Cambridge, 1954), p. 13.

Here the scientist finds a widespread unawareness of his predicament. There is a persistent and legitimate appeal for what Sir Ifor Evans has called 'a wider act of interpretation' by scientists.[1] Some, notably J. B. S. Haldane and J. Z. Young in recent times, and Sir Arthur Eddington and Sir Charles Sherrington of an earlier generation, have responded to the appeal. But it must be remembered that it takes the scientist perhaps twenty or thirty years to reach full confidence and proficiency in his scientific dialect and that mature grasp of his subject which enables him to see it clearly both in depth and in relation to other disciplines. This proficiency he can acquire only by single-handed devotion to his scientific work and at the cost of some withdrawal from the affairs of everyday life. The double combination of full proficiency in a scientific dialect with sympathetic appreciation of the layman's need, together with the skill to interpret the dialect and the desire to do so, is rare indeed. And full proficiency, full authority is all-important for the interpreter of science. Only the pre-eminent scientist can make simple unqualified scientific statements acceptable to scientists and laymen alike. Similar simple statements could be made by men of lesser repute only at the risk of imperilling their scientific reputations. Only at the pre-eminent stage of his career can the scientist achieve the simplicity of wisdom.

It has also to be understood that the layman often demands more than it is possible for the scientist to give. As J. Z. Young says, 'Those who cannot use mathematics are disqualified from "observing" electrons.'[2] The personal experience of a life-time of research cannot be expressed in the few hundred words which would provide the layman with a half-hour of reading by his fireside. The best of translations from scientific dialects into everyday language can give only a glimmer of what the scientist is doing. Words are a poor substitute for experience. If the humanist really wants to *understand* science he must be ready to make the effort to understand the scientific dialects by sharing

[1] *Literature and Science* (London, 1954), p. 113.
[2] *Doubt and Certainty in Science* (Oxford, 1951), p. 123.

the scientist's experience in the laboratory, to make an effort comparable with that which he has devoted to his own humanistic studies. There is no short cut to full understanding. Lamb's *Tales from Shakespeare* are not Shakespeare.

My cursory glance at the field in which the scientist works and writes must end with one further observation on practical writing, the reports and the memoranda on which industry and commerce depend: that is, that despite its many faults, it works. It performs its multiplicity of functions, even if inefficiently at times. If we intercept a letter, a paper, or a report, between the writer and the reader, we can always detect some fault to complain of. But release it to complete its mission, and generally that mission will be seen to have been accomplished. It is very difficult indeed to find a document so badly written that it has led to serious error. There is an obvious reason for this. If the mistake is detectable, if it can be pointed out and corrected, then the mistake can be allowed for. In practice, it is allowed for, though the effort of making the mental correction can be distracting and irritating.

The windscreen of a motor car provides an analogy. Normally the driver looks through the windscreen at the road beyond, keeping his eye on possible sources of interference with his progress and adjusting his speed and direction as circumstances require. If the road is dirty, his windscreen will become spotted with mud. He may be half aware of the spots of mud and yet be able to see through them and between them to the road ahead. He will be able to drive at his normal speed with no risk. The time may come, of course, when the windscreen is so bespattered that it would be dangerous to continue without stopping, to clean it; but this is a rare occurrence. It would also be dangerous if the driver became so obsessed with the spots of mud on the screen that he focused on them alone; again, he would no longer see where he was going. I sometimes think that teachers of English, and others, become obsessed with the spots of mud. I know that it would be better to keep the windscreen perfectly clean. But most car drivers and most readers of English will look through the mud to the road beyond. Without stopping to clean the windscreen as every spot appears, or correcting every mistake they find, they will continue their journey and reach their destination.

Recently, a first-year Hungarian student, discussing his experience of this country, told me that he liked the English and that they had been kind to him. But he made one significant reservation: 'My English is not yet good,' he said, 'so English people never listen to *what* I say, they only correct the way I say it.'

IV

This brings me to the third major topic I want to discuss—the teacher's attitude to, or theory of, language and teaching. This is not a theory that one teaches, but one which intellectually justifies one's teaching methods. I think that it would be generally agreed that if the theory underlying the teaching is at fault, then the teaching practice based on it will also be at fault.

The main difficulty in discussing this important matter is that the theory underlying language teaching is rarely made explicit. I cannot refer you to any work in which it is made plain. It seems to be so firmly embedded in our language and attitudes that it can no longer be seen. I can only infer what it is from the speech and teaching practice that I observe. There are two aspects of the theory to be considered: the first is the conflict between analysis and synthesis which confronts every teacher, and especially the teacher of English, and the second is the teacher's view of the nature of language itself.

In every academic subject the scholar either surveys his chosen field and then begins to analyse it, or he continues an analysis already begun, or he rejects all earlier analyses and makes a new one. Analysis is the first duty of the scholar and the instrument with which he works. He breaks down his chosen field into as many discriminable bits and pieces as he can and seeks their inter-relations. There may be more than one analysis that serves the scholar's purpose of making enlightening correlations between the fragments of his subject; or there may be one analysis which, for a time, becomes established as the most 'natural' or fruitful. The history of science shows clearly the adoption and rejection of successively deeper and more fruitful analyses. It justifies a remark quoted by Maurois that 'if the first duty of a scholar is to invent a system, his second is to regard it with disgust',[1] and Oppenheimer's more forthright statement that 'it is the business of science to be wrong'.[2]

The scholar then hands over his analysis to the teacher who in turn has the task of presenting his subject in a form that his young pupils, unable to see the unity that is being analysed, can digest, persuading them to accept the bits and pieces in the hope that they will eventually synthesize them. When the bits and pieces are 'synthesized' by the pupil, then not only can he analyse them as required at the request of the teacher but he can also recognize at once the situations in which they are applicable and apply them. In arithmetic, for example, the pupil who has achieved a synthesis of his multiplication tables can solve practical 'problems' which involve their use.

The analysis can be communicated; that is to say, the bits and pieces can be clearly presented one at a time by word, by diagram, and the usual teaching techniques. They can be inculcated by rote or by drill; they can be isolated and listed as items in a syllabus. But the synthesis cannot be communicated, cannot be taught directly. If the synthesis is achieved at all, it is done only by the pupils individually. All that the teacher can do is to encourage them to make the necessary effort and to persuade them, perhaps by his own example and enthusiasm for his subject, that the synthesis he has achieved is worth striving for.

The teacher is helped in this difficult task by the fact that the young human, as any other organism, is a born synthesizer. He 'puts two and two together' whether you want him to or not. But what he puts together, or *can* put together, is not necessarily

[1] *Un Art de Vivre* (Paris, 1939), p. 33.

[2] Reported by I. A. Richards, *Speculative Instruments* (London, 1955), p. 174.

what the teacher offers him. Those bits that fit into the synthesis he has already achieved—'schemata' is the current word—may be accepted, but those that do not fit, or easily adhere, pass him by. Eddington has an analogy of a net lowered into the sea.[1] The fish that are caught depend on the size and shape of the mesh. But the fisherman believes always that his catch is typical of the fish that are there, and lowers his net to catch more of the same kind. The task of the teacher is to assess the state of the individual schemata of the pupils in front of him, to present such items of his analysed subject that he thinks might adhere or be entrapped in the mesh, and to coax the developing schemata in the direction in which he hopes to guide his pupils towards a synthesis. Every synthesizing step the individual makes is his own personal discovery: any attempt to force a particular synthesis inhibits it. Education, thus seen, is a system of providing the young with an environment in which they are encouraged to make their own intellectual discoveries. Described thus in my metaphors the task of the teacher sounds easy, but all teachers know how incredibly difficult, how much a hit-and-miss affair it is. There are few rules, methods, techniques that can be recommended with confidence; while the teacher is precariously fumbling his way, learning to interpret the reactions of his pupils, there they sit steadily synthesizing a random and unknown selection of all the multifarious bits and pieces that come their way.

But one thing is certain. To teach a subject simply by presenting the young pupils with the fragments that result from the penetrating analysis of generations of scholars is unlikely to be effective, though this is what we often try to do. Professor Quirk, in the first essay of this volume, emphasized the need for the study of grammar and literature to go hand in hand. The teacher of English is generally, I believe, more aware of the danger than are most of his colleagues. He, more than any other teacher, is confronted with the need to judge, from his intuitive assessment

[1] *The Philosophy of Physical Science* (Cambridge, 1949), pp. 16 ff. Eddington develops the analogy to illustrate 'subjective selection'.

of the attitudes and degrees of linguistic synthesis his pupils have attained, what further quantum of analysed material they can profit from. It is the English teacher who meets this problem in its most acute form: Mr Mittins refers to the phases of intellectual growth which Whitehead distinguishes in children—of romance, precision, and generalization—phases that occur later in science than in the humanities. The success or failure of the English teacher is the main determinant in deciding the academic careers of his pupils; those who succeed with him can choose the humanities or the sciences; while those who fail are debarred from the study of the humanities.

So the teacher of English must tread very delicately indeed. If I am more conscious of the failures of English teaching than of its successes, it is because the only students I now see are engineers or scientists. The English teacher can legitimately take pride in the successes; but I do not hold him solely responsible for the failures, because he does not get from his colleagues the support that his subject demands. English is the key to all school subjects, including other languages and science, but if schoolchildren observe that it is important only during the English class while the physicist, the chemist, the mathematician, and possibly others, have no apparent regard for it whatever, they are apt to 'put two and two together' again. It is outside the English classroom that the pupil can exercise his English in a natural though informal way, acquiring vocabulary and making the new discriminations demanded by his learning of the particulars. It is here that the English lesson can be applied. But all this needs the active interest and co-operation of his fellow-teachers. Does the English teacher get it?

I have some disturbing questions to ask, questions which I cannot answer from my own experience. Is it true that in marking G.C.E. papers in physics or chemistry, let us say, the examiner merely skips over the scripts, not reading them, but merely scanning them in the hope of detecting those significant formulae, equations, diagrams, enunciations of laws, and definitions for which the marks have been allotted by the examining panel?

Is it true that semi-illiterate scripts in English Literature are marked in the same way? Is it true that it has become necessary to set Scholarship level candidates, whatever their main subject, a specially designed paper in what is called 'The *Use* of English'? If so, may I ask what it is that is being used in the physics papers, the English Literature, and other papers? Or is the 'Use of English' something different from the use of English? Whatever the answers to these questions may be, to many children English is what is 'done' in the English class—and nowhere else does it seem to be needed. It must look very odd to them.

V

The second aspect of the teacher's theory I want to comment on is his view of the nature of language. Clearly a fault here will lead to faults of teaching. Most people, I believe, if pressed to describe the process that goes on between a lecturer and his audience, would use the Platonic terminology of 'ideas' or 'thoughts'. In its simplest version the description would run thus: 'the lecturer has certain ideas or thoughts that he wishes to convey to them. He clothes the thoughts in words and utters them in the conventional forms of English. The sounds impinge on their ears and by the action of their aural nervous systems and the associated parts of their brains, the words are stripped from his utterance and the naked thought falls into place in their minds. Thus his thoughts or ideas have been conveyed from his mind to theirs.' A more sophisticated, pseudo-scientific version of the same description uses the language of information theory. It would run: 'the lecturer has information to transmit to them. He encodes this information in appropriate speech signals and transmits his signals orally. They receive the signals and (disregarding possible interference by "noise") they decode them and thus come to possess the information he wishes to transmit.' It will be agreed that both versions imply that something, either 'thoughts' or 'ideas' or 'information', passes between the participants.

This theory, with minor variants, is widely held. It is embedded in our language and in our educational system. I think it arises because for over two thousand years we have taken too narrow a view of language. If you can abstract all utterance from the context in which it is made and study it intensively, attending only to the dead words lying before you, dissecting them, analysing them, holding them up to the light, putting them under the microscope, then you may learn much about dead words. But any theories you propound about living words are likely to be unreliable. It is rather like trying to discover how people live and behave solely by the method of killing them and examining their corpses. One cause of the trouble is the fatal ease with which the words themselves can be isolated and the rest ignored; the second cause is the belief implicit in the Platonic theory that the linguistic part of any communicative process is the whole of it.

The Platonic theory that I am criticizing cannot be refuted by recourse to logic because *applied* logic is part of it; nor can it be refuted by any other form of linguistic analysis employed by philosophers because that also is part of it. 'Philosophical problems arise when language goes on holiday', wrote Ludwig Wittgenstein.[1] The theory is refuted only by observing that human behaviour does not conform with what the theory predicts. Here I can indicate only some of the consequences of holding the theory which are relevant now. The teacher who believes that a quantum of information passes from A to B whenever he speaks also believes that his teaching duty is performed if he prepares careful notes for his class or lecture and delivers his material in a firm clear voice. By this means the thoughts he has chosen to impart are conveyed to the minds of his pupils. If he were to set a test after his lecture to see how many of his thoughts had actually reached them he might be disappointed. But he could always explain poor results away by claiming that his students were inattentive or tired or in some other way to blame.

Such a teacher, too, would regard knowledge as the positivist

[1] *Philosophical Investigations* (Oxford, 1953), p. 19.

does—as a great heap of facts, thoughts, ideas, piled up in some metaphysical limbo; he would take it for granted that such facts could be shovelled about, imprisoned in books or rammed down students' throats. He would regard examination marks as though they indicated depth of knowledge rather as a dip-stick indicates the depth of water in a tank. He would draw up minutely detailed syllabuses of instruction and tick off the items one by one as they were 'done'. He would teach English grammar and other analytical subjects, by the repercussive method.

But most teachers, even if they pay lip-service to the Platonic theory, are, of course, compelled in practice to modify their attitude to it when they are confronted by the inarticulate cussedness of the human young. I am reminded of the story of the swimming instructor who lined up his class of children for their first swimming lesson. 'Watch me!' he said, plunging into the bath and swimming around. 'This is the breast stroke', and he demonstrated it, 'this the back stroke, and this the crawl. Right, now you jump in and swim.' They jumped, but did not swim. It was quite obvious to the instructor that they had not been attending. It is quite obvious to us that he would have to modify his methods. When action based on theory and analysis patently fails in human affairs, then action, guided by an intuitive and sensitive response to the situation, can sometimes succeed. But the Platonic theory is widely and firmly held in high academic circles—more firmly as the holder removes himself from the communicative difficulties of the classroom. This is not surprising. The Platonic theory offers an adequate metaphorical description of the communicative process that occurs between human beings of largely similar experience, attitude, and outlook. It breaks down where it is most needed—when the experience of those who wish to communicate with each other is dissimilar and disparate, between young and old, between humanist and scientist, between teacher and pupil.

If we summarily dismiss the Platonic theory I have criticized, then, you may ask, what do we put in its place? The answer is that we need no substitute. Any substitute would be the same theory in a new cloak. All I suggest is that, if the Platonic terminology is now discarded, many spurious problems immediately evaporate and our real communicative and teaching problems, obscured at present in a fog of misty words, become more clearly discernible.

If I had to describe the process that occurs in a lecture, all I could say at present is this: though communication takes place, nothing is communicated. A speaker addresses someone, and displays himself—mainly, but not wholly, by uttering words. One attends to his display and interprets it in the light of one's experience of similar situations. Nothing is communicated. There is only a display, and private interpretations of it.

Colleagues in the fields of psychology, anatomy, physiology, physics, phonetics, and in language departments, can amplify my simple description with more details of this complex process. But, for the practical purposes of the classroom and other personal communication in everyday life, my simple metaphorical description is at present all we have to work on. It awaits analysis. At least it has the merit of making plain our ignorance of how the communicative process works.

Of course, it takes a long time to adjust oneself to a different way of looking at language. But here is a simple test that can be applied. Note your reaction to this statement by James Joyce: 'The demand that I make of my reader is that he devote his whole life to reading my works.' [1] If you find that a presumptuous demand, then you have not yet shaken off your heritage of Platonic metaphysics; if you are able to regard it as a platitude, you probably have.

VI

Now I shall turn to the course I give to third-year electrical engineering students. Any teaching such as mine has to satisfy

[1] Max Eastman, *The Literary Mind: its Place in an Age of Science* (New York, 1931), p. 100. This remark of Joyce's was made in an interview with Eastman (who does not interpret it as it is interpreted here).

five conditions. The first is that in this age of rapid technological advance new topics clamour for inclusion in any engineering or science course faster than old topics can be discarded. My teaching must therefore take a subservient place and must be designed to offer the best return for the least distraction from normal studies. The second condition is that you cannot teach writing simply by talking—remember the story of the swimming bath. The third is that my course must not claim to teach 'English'. Although most students are well aware of their linguistic deficiencies and are privately anxious to remedy them, the legacy of the history I outlined earlier coupled with the students' antipathy to anything that reminds them of the English lessons of their schooldays means that any claim to teach 'English' would be met by passive resistance or worse. That is a sad but empirical fact. I teach very little English as 'teaching English' is generally understood; and the little I do is in the main incidental. Yet I think that the results of the course in what we call the Presentation of Technical Information is broadly what the teacher of English would hope to achieve.

The fourth condition is imposed by the very wide range of linguistic attainment likely to be found in a class of engineers or scientists. They are not usually segregated by examinations into a homogeneous class with roughly similar linguistic attainment in the same way as they are segregated for their normal subjects. I find that some private teaching of individuals is essential. The fifth condition that a teacher of English to science and engineering students has to meet is that they are mainly interested in their engineering or science, so that any course of writing must be closely related to their main interests. There have been attempts elsewhere to save the scientist from the taint of illiteracy by giving him a course in English literature or poetry. If such courses are well done I am sure that some students are helped by them. But they are luxuries, because there is no guarantee that science and engineering students will make for themselves the link between literature or poetry and their science: there is no guarantee that they will be able to make the synthesis that I believe is essential. They will become scientists who know a little poetry or literature. My approach is frankly utilitarian—I try to teach them to write better reports. *Better* reports? This implies making value-judgements about engineering reports or scientific papers. Yes, value-judgements about literature—*scientific* literature. And why not? This is the only literature these students are interested in and which they can fully understand and appreciate. This literature lies wholly or almost wholly within their experience. A scientific report *to the scientist* can be original, creative, imaginative, profound, elegant, in precisely the same aesthetic sense as these words are used by the man of letters. The scientific paper is the scientist's mode of expression. I know that non-scientists may not appreciate this point—I have quoted the criticisms of some of them. But, as Proust put it: 'True distinction always affects to address only distinguished persons who know the same customs, and it doesn't explain! A book of Anatole France implies a host of learned knowledge, including unending allusions that the herd does not perceive there, and these, its other beauties apart, make up its incomparable nobility.'[1] In the same way a scientific paper, or even an engineering report, can be regarded as a literary art form and is so regarded by those 'who know the same customs' and who can recognize the 'unending allusions' to other scientific works. The main difference between the scientist and the man of letters is that the scientist does not normally make explicit, let alone publicize, his aesthetic emotions; there are no schools of scientific literature, no critics, no professors of scientific literature to encourage him to do so. After reading a great science book or paper the scientist quietly returns with new zest and new insight to his bench, as the writer, after a similar experience, returns refreshed to his desk.

In short, I claim that a purely utilitarian approach can establish for the scientist or engineering student the basis of an aesthetic judgement which is soundly rooted in his own experience and understanding. Moreover, I find that as soon as he has established his criteria for scientific works he begins to transfer them to other

[1] *Pastiches et Mélanges* (Paris, 1919), p. 266 *n.*

art forms in which he happens to be interested. He feels confidence in his own judgement, no longer asking the prudential question, 'What *ought* I to think?' The link has been made and the synthesis has begun.

Now for details of the course: I begin by persuading the students to purge their vocabularies of the clichés, woolly phrases, and tired words and to write in a simple plain style. They sometimes complain that I have left them nothing to write with, but it would be more correct for them to admit that they have, at this stage, nothing to say. When the purge is complete they are left with a plain naked style, free or almost free from grammatical faults; but it is dull and pedestrian. I then allow them to relax and encourage them to write more fluently according to their individual tastes. I encourage them to experiment and to acquire a versatility of style appropriate to different occasions and readers.

I do very little correcting. Exercises are brought to me in private tutorials. I read them quietly but audibly with the student at my side. I try as honestly as I can to read them as communications rather than as exercises, not looking for trouble but driving ahead without worrying about the spots on the windscreen. The student observes my natural reactions as I read and soon learns politely to flick the spots of mud from the windscreen as they appear—*he* makes the corrections, not I. Then we talk about *what* has been said and the student can verify for himself how well he has told me what he intended. That, I think, is the limit of my direct English teaching.

We also consider the structure of reports and papers in detail. I encourage the students to look at a report as a unity and to assess to what extent it meets its intended purpose—to look through the windscreen even if it is muddy and to enjoy the journey. From our narrow utilitarian point of view the most serious faults of a scientific paper are not linguistic defects but irrelevancies of 'matter'. If he has to make the choice the practical man much prefers crudely expressed relevance to elegantly expressed irrelevance. The teacher must never imply that it is

F

more important to make statements correctly than to select the correct statements to make.

I give about fifteen lectures. The main topics are in this order: communication in the widest sense; language and vocabulary in scientific writing; the relation of formal and informal logical systems to language and to science; definition; explanation and description; the use and misuse of analogy. The lectures are not formal. I like them to 'degenerate' into discussion as soon as possible. Communication, if my view is correct, is not a one-way process but a sequential alternation of display and responding display, or an interplay of what I. A. Richards calls 'feed-forward'[1] with what engineers call 'feed-back'.

The exercises I set are short but demand some care. A student's exercise fails only when it bores me. The course culminates for the student in the writing of a report of about 5,000 words on a minor research problem. He devotes one term's practical work and reading to this task and when he has finished this he finds, usually for the first time in his life, that, as an engineer, he has something new to say about engineering and he wants to say it. For the first time he *wants* to write. At last he feels that he has the only possible justification for writing—something to say. And he begins to have respect for those who can write well.

I have described not a *method* of teaching English but a personal solution to a particular problem, a 'fragment of an autobiography'. I believe that the study of 'communication', the modern hob-nailed substitute for Day Lewis's 'magic', could, if we wished, make poetry and science one again.

[1] *Speculative Instruments* (London, 1955), p. 119.

CHAPTER 7

The teaching of English as a foreign language | *J. C. Catford*

I

In the first essay of this volume, Professor Quirk emphasizes the need for the 'study of language in linguistic terms' (p. 12), and the relevance of this to all branches of English study. I shall try below to develop that theme a little in relation to the special field of teaching English as a foreign language. But before I reach that point, I should like to make a wider survey of my subject.

The teaching of English or of any language as a foreign language may be described as a process of creating bilinguals. I am using the word 'bilingual' here as a technical term meaning any person who can and does make alternate use of more than one language or dialect.[1] In everyday speech the word 'bilingual' generally refers to a person who has virtually *equal* command of two or more languages. If a special term is required for such persons of equal linguistic skill (which is very difficult to measure) I should prefer to call them 'ambilinguals'. Ambilinguals are relatively rare. For most bilinguals, one language is dominant, or primary; other languages are secondary. One may, for convenience, use the abbreviation 'L1' for primary language, and

[1] Cf. U. Weinreich, *Languages in Contact* (New York, 1953), p. 1, and the reports on 'Languages in Contact' by E. Haugen and U. Weinreich in *Proceedings of the Eighth International Congress of Linguists* (Oslo, 1958), pp. 771–95. Strictly speaking, the alternate use of more than two languages is 'multilingualism' and the persons involved are 'multilingual' (adj.) or 'multilinguals' (n.).

'L2' for secondary language.[1] L1 is usually, but not always, the language first acquired in childhood; it is the language of its speaker's intimate everyday life; it is also to a large extent the language of counting and other forms of verbal self-stimulation, or 'thinking in words'. Most people—that is all except perhaps ambilinguals—have only one L1, but they may have a number of L2's, each perhaps being reserved for one particular purpose, as, for instance, reading scientific papers, enjoying a Mediterranean holiday, reading the scriptures.

The teaching of English as a secondary language, then, is the process of creating English-using bilinguals (not, usually, ambilinguals), and the problems involved, and the principles underlying this process, are different from those relating to the teaching of English to native speakers of English.

On the other hand, the teaching of English as L2 is not a fundamentally different problem from the teaching of any other secondary language. As the late Professor Gatenby has pointed out,[2] the tendency to isolate every foreign language for special treatment has been a hindrance to the spread of information concerning foreign language study. 'Yet', he goes on to say, 'second language teaching as an art or science is in its main principles universal, like every other art or science, however great the variety may be in materials and conditions.' It is important to place the teaching of English as L2 in the wider context of secondary language teaching in general.

The necessity for some people to learn secondary languages must be almost as old as Babel, and the systematic teaching of languages is certainly of a respectable antiquity. It might not be straining the facts too far to say that our oldest grammar of a secondary language is the Sanskrit grammar of Pāninī, which was written in perhaps the fourth century B.C. In Pāninī's time, no

[1] I prefer these abbreviations to Weinreich's P-language and S-language, as in 'On the Description of Phonic Interference', *Word*, vol. 13 (1957), because I should like to reserve SL for 'source language' (as against TL, 'target language') in discussion about translation.

[2] In *English Language Teaching*, vol. 4 (1949–50), p. 146.

doubt, the colloquial Prakrits of Northern India were not widely different from the Sanskrit which he described, but his grammar has remained in use down to the present day, when Sanskrit is undoubtedly a secondary language for all those who learn it.

In spite of the antiquity of secondary language teaching there is remarkably little certainty about the best way of doing it. Professor Gatenby, in the article already quoted (p. 144), is being somewhat optimistic when he says 'the strange thing is that though the problems connected with language learning were all known and solved more than one hundred years ago the solutions have never been given widespread acceptance or application'. It is true that many techniques which are used today have been tried in the past and several have been 'rediscovered' more than once. Nevertheless, there is anything but agreement even on fundamental questions. Should the approach to language learning always be an oral one, for instance, or should the emphasis be on reading in the initial stages? It seems obvious that this must depend on circumstances, on the aims of a particular course. Yet there is disagreement about this, and there is a powerful body of opinion in favour of an initial oral approach in all circumstances. But the validity of this has been questioned,[1] and my colleague Dennis Ward, Head of the Russian Department of the University of Edinburgh, has organized a highly successful course in Russian for scientists, which keeps the oral aspects of the language down to an absolute minimum.

Again, wherein lies the greatest difficulty in L2 learning? Henry Sweet was in no doubt about this: 'The fact that the languages commonly learnt by Europeans belong mostly to the same Aryan stock, and have besides a large vocabulary in common of borrowed Latin, French, and Greek words, is apt to blind them to a recognition of the fact that the real intrinsic difficulty of learning a foreign language lies in that of having to master its vocabulary.'[2] Charles C. Fries is equally positive:

[1] Notably by D. Abercrombie, *Problems and Principles* (London, 1956), pp. 21-3.

[2] *The Practical Study of Languages* (London, 1899), p. 66.

'In learning a new language . . . the chief problem is not at first that of learning vocabulary items. It is, first, the mastery of the sound system—to understand the stream of speech, to hear the distinctive sound features and to approximate their production. It is, second, the mastery of the features of arrangement that constitute the structure of the language.'[1]

Uncertainties and differences of opinion are not surprising in view of the complexity of the task and the variety of problems and factors involved. 'Learning is a complicated process', writes Harold Dunkel,[2] 'and the study of it has been an increasingly important and vigorous branch of psychology. Language too involves an array of intricate problems, especially those concerning the relation of language to personality and thought. In language learning, where the complexities of both language and learning must be handled simultaneously, the problems we confront are usually those which are the most baffling of each field individually. . . . In view of this situation, the odds are certainly against our knowing much about the teaching or learning of a second language.' Nevertheless, as he goes on to say: 'Despite these complications some language teachers appear fully convinced that they have the answers and that if everyone would adopt their theories and procedures (or better yet, their textbooks), there would be no further trouble.'

Many of these theories and procedures have been crystallized in what are known as 'Methods'—either because they have been so called by their sponsors, or because they have been taken up and developed (or else criticized and condemned) by others, and language teachers have a remarkable tendency to confer the title of 'Method' on any procedures which seem to answer some of their needs. Thus we have, or have had, 'The Grammar-Translation Method', 'The Natural Method', 'The Psychological Method', 'The Reform or Phonetic Method', 'The Direct Method', 'The Oral Method or Approach', 'The Reading Method', 'The New Method', 'The Eclectic or Compromise

[1] *Teaching and Learning English as a Foreign Language* (Ann Arbor, 1945), p. 3.
[2] *Second-Language Learning* (Boston, 1948), p. 1.

Method',[1] and, latterly, procedures used in the Division of Language Teaching at the University of London Institute of Education have come to be widely known, without this being the intention of their originators, as 'The Method of Graded Structures' or 'The Structural Approach'.[2] The trouble about this canonizing of procedures is that once something has been labelled 'The X Method', it is often assumed to be the answer to all problems and to be applicable under all circumstances, in all L2 teaching operations. But there are so many variable factors involved in L2 teaching that it would be surprising if any one 'method' were appropriate to all circumstances: and again, any really complete 'method' must be concerned with the whole range of teaching problems.[3]

II

I can do little more here than hint at some of the complexities of L2 teaching. Any language teaching operation takes place in a context of highly variable external factors, and must be adjusted to suit them. Some of these factors are:

(a) the geographical situation, political affiliations, and economic conditions of the country where the teaching is being carried on;

[1] For a brief description of these 'Methods', see, for example, T. K. N. Menon and M. S. Patel, *The Teaching of English as a Foreign Language* (Baroda, 1957), ch. 5-7, and J. O. Gauntlett, *Teaching English as a Foreign Language* (London, 1957), ch. 2.

[2] It must be noted that this 'Structural Approach' is quite different from that which is referred to in the title of the first essay in this volume. Professor Quirk, of course, is talking about the approach to the scientific study of language which is known as 'structural linguistics'. The teaching method which I am here referring to is one which lays stress on the careful grading of grammatical items. It is unfortunate that these items are sometimes all referred to indiscriminately as 'structures' whether they are, in fact, 'constructions', or simply specific items such as particular tenses, pronouns, etc.

[3] Cf. W. F. Mackey's valuable article, 'The Meaning of Method', *English Language Teaching*, vol. 5 (1950-1), p. 3, and his subsequent articles on 'Selection', ibid., vol. 7 (1952-3), p. 77, 'Grading', ibid., vol. 8 (1953-4), p. 45, and 'Presentation', ibid., vol. 9 (1954-5), p. 41.

(b) the internal linguistic situation in that country (for example, is there one or more than one national language? Is the national language a 'world language' or a purely local language? Is there a large number of regional or minority languages? What uses are actually made of the particular L2 we are interested in?);

(c) the student's age, intelligence, educational and cultural background, motivation, etc.;

(d) the teacher's training, experience, cultural background, etc.;

(e) characteristics of L2;

(f) characteristics of L1, and, especially, differences between L1 and L2.

The planning of any L2 teaching operation—the design of any 'method'—should take at least these factors into account. Some of them, such as the general conditions and the linguistic conditions in the country concerned, will influence overall policy. English can be taught largely as a 'humanistic' or 'cultural' subject in a Western European country such as France. In other countries, such as India or Pakistan, English may be primarily needed as an essential instrument of practical everyday life in certain spheres of activity (as, for instance, telecommunications, commerce, technology, higher education). Some of the other factors, especially those relating to the student and to the particular languages involved, (c), (e), (f), will influence planning in a more detailed way.

Moreover, the design of a 'method' involves at least three distinct kinds of planning. These may be termed 'Selection', 'Grading', and 'Presentation': Selection, because obviously not everything can be taught at once, and a decision must be made as to what to include in a language course; Grading, or the process of deciding what to teach before what, how much of each item to bring in at each step and so on; and Presentation, or the way in which the material which has been selected and graded is to be put before the pupils. Moreover, these three operations must be applied to all aspects of the language being taught —its pronunciation, grammar, vocabulary, and the texts or situations within which the material will be presented and practised.

Not only are these operations dependent on the more external factors listed earlier, but they are to some extent interdependent. Thus, the type of Presentation which is envisaged must to some extent influence Selection and Grading. For example, if the intention is that in the early stages the material is to be presented orally, largely as verbal accompaniments to actions performed in the classroom, then it will probably be advisable to introduce the so-called 'present continuous' tense at an early stage, before the 'simple present'. Thus, 'What am I doing? I'm going to the blackboard. I'm writing on the blackboard.' If, on the other hand, the presentation is to be largely in the form of written texts, the 'simple present' may well be introduced first, in narratives of this kind: 'John is a boy. He lives in London. He goes to school every day.'

Selection, Grading, and Presentation, as I have said, are applicable to all aspects of the language. The principle of vocabulary selection and grading is now widely recognized.[1] The careful selection and grading of grammatical items is also practised by many modern text-book writers, though this aspect of the problem has so far received much less attention than the selection and grading of vocabulary.

The selection and grading of pronunciation items is still often left to chance: this is frequently assumed to be inevitable. Or the problem is simply ignored. In one sense, however, selection of pronunciation is forced from the start upon every text-book

[1] Vocabulary selection, as is well known, is most commonly based on frequency counts. This is not the only, nor necessarily the best, basis of selection. The principles underlying the vocabulary selection for Basic English are different, and for some purposes, more valuable. Cf. J. C. Catford 'Intelligibility', *English Language Teaching*, vol. 5 (1950–1), and 'The Background and Origins of Basic English', ibid. For recent work on vocabulary and grammar selection for the teaching of French, see Gougenheim, Michéa, Rivenc, and Sauvageot, *L'élaboration du français élémentaire* (Paris, 1957).

writer or teacher concerned with spoken English. He must at least decide whether to use an American or British variety of English,[1] and this decision is likely to be influenced by political and geographical considerations. Neither form of English has any intrinsic superiority. Within each of these broad types there are several acceptable varieties. If the broad choice is to be British (and I include here certain Commonwealth varieties) the more specific choice may well be 'RP' (Received Pronunciation, the type of pronunciation described by Daniel Jones in his *Outline of English Phonetics*, and used in his *English Pronouncing Dictionary*). But, as D. Abercrombie has pointed out,[2] there are other varieties which are equally acceptable—for example, Scots or Irish or some Commonwealth forms of English. In the last resort, however, the matter is usually decided by practical considerations such as the pronunciation of the teacher, or any other available model, and the type of pronunciation described or exemplified in accessible text-books or works of reference. In British books, this is usually RP.

Another procedure would be to apply as rigorous selection to pronunciation as to vocabulary: in other words, to teach a systematically *restricted* form of English pronunciation, which would be reasonably intelligible for purposes of international communication, but which would be specially tailored to fit the phonetic capabilities of learners with a particular L1 background. This is an approach which has not so far been fully explored, but which is perfectly feasible.[3]

The selection of literary texts is another question. In his essay in this volume Mr Mittins endorses Professor Quirk's view, that the teaching of language needs literature as its prime material. In the context of L2 teaching, 'literature' raises special problems. One of these is purely linguistic. Up to a certain stage in a graded course, it is obvious that 'real literature' must be ruled out. But there comes a point in a general-purpose course when it is

[1] This decision, of course, affects grammar and vocabulary as well.
[2] *Problems and Principles*, p. 53.
[3] Ibid., pp. 37-9.

desirable to introduce literature,[1] and, particularly with adult students, the reading of 'the real thing' in the original may be an exciting experience and a powerful stimulus to further effort. But, as Jespersen has remarked,[2] one needs to know a foreign language pretty well in order to get more out of the original than out of a translation.

The other problem is cultural, rather than linguistic: it involves the question of cultural difficulty and cultural grading. The understanding of the literature of an L2 demands some understanding of the cultural background, the cultural context, of the language and its literature. Conversely, knowledge of the cultural context is a help in learning the language. Cultural difficulty and linguistic difficulty are not necessarily correlated. A Shakespeare play, for example, may be linguistically difficult for many foreigners (as, indeed, it is for native speakers of English), but, if it deals largely with general human values and situations, it may be simpler from the cultural point of view than a work of Galsworthy's, for instance, which is deeply embedded in an English cultural matrix. We need lists of English literary texts graded culturally as well as linguistically.

In a preliminary experiment on this subject, I have given short passages from Shakespeare, Aldous Huxley, Jane Austen, Leo Walmsley, and George Orwell to a group of foreign specialists in the teaching of English and asked them to comment on the relative cultural difficulty of the various passages. The result was much as one would expect. The Shakespeare passage, from *Macbeth*, apart from linguistic difficulties, proved relatively easy from the cultural point of view, but passages from Orwell's *Down and Out in Paris and London* and Walmsley's *The Golden Waterwheel* contained many references to Western European or specifically English culture that were regarded as likely to be baffling to Indian, Indonesian, or Japanese readers.

---

[1] The texts used in, for example, a science reading course will naturally be scientific writing rather than 'literature' in the usual sense, though the two are, of course, not mutually exclusive.

[2] *How to Teach a Foreign Language* (London, 1904), p. 5.

These, then, are some of the complex circumstances and some of the problems of secondary language teaching. Because of the number of variables involved, it is extremely difficult to make controlled experiments in this field, and there is, in consequence, remarkably little reliable evidence about the relative value of different procedures. Much of the published discussion of the subject consists of little more than claim and counter-claim based on personal opinion and experience. New developments in language teaching must always be endorsed by the personal experience of practical teachers. But, just because such experience *is* personal and limited, it can rarely have universal validity: after all, the personality of the teacher is itself an important variable in the language teaching situation. For guidance in certain aspects of the problem, and for principles of general validity, we must, at times, turn to the disciplines which are concerned with the scientific study of *learning* on the one hand and of *language* on the other—to psychology and linguistics.

III

'The study of language in linguistic terms' exerts a useful guiding influence in nearly all aspects of L2 teaching. The social function of language, criteria of 'correctness', the relationships between 'vernaculars' and 'koinês' or official languages, the uses of specific L2's, the study of restricted languages, bilingualism and language contact, the 'meaning of meaning', the theory and practice of translation—all these are, in part at least, questions for the linguist. In addition, linguistics has particular contributions to make in at least two spheres. These are, first, in the comparison of L1 and L2, and secondly, in the provision of an adequate description of L2; for no amount of careful Selection, Grading, and Presentation will be effective, if it is based on a description which is inadequate.

That comparison of L1 with L2 provides important background material in secondary language teaching is fairly widely recognized. Indeed, it seems self-evident that interference from the mother-tongue or from previously learned secondary languages is one of the basic difficulties in learning a new language. It is particularly noticeable in pronunciation. The Japanese, for instance, have enormous difficulty with English pronunciation, because the syllabic structure and sound-systems of Japanese are very different from those of English. Germans, on the other hand, have less difficulty because of somewhat greater phonological similarity with English.

But even similarities can be treacherous. That this is so in respect of vocabulary, at least, is well known. The French *actuellement* is not the same as English *actually*, and the Russian *genial'ny* ('of genius') is not the same as English *genial*. I remember being momentarily surprised at seeing Stalin's article, 'Marxism and Linguistics', referred to in a Russian journal as what looked at first sight like 'the genial work of J. V. Stalin'.

The importance of L1 interference in L2 training is sometimes minimized. For instance, the author of a well-known book on common errors in English goes out of his way to argue that most such errors are due to other causes, such as misplaced zeal on the part of the student, or the 'illogicalities' of English. But the evidence he advances in support of this view does not stand up to examination. After presenting a large number of common errors which are said to be found all over the world, he goes on: 'The argument here presented is that if errors are due, as unmistakably as the best authorities would have us believe, to cross-association' (that is, L1 interference), 'then the Japanese form of error should be one thing and the Bantu form quite another. But the plain fact is that Japanese and Bantu alike say "Yes, I didn't", and they have scores of other errors in common.'[1] The 'plain fact', however, is that this particular example, which is given as crucial, contradicts the argument. There are many languages in which affirmation and denial of the 'yes' or 'no' type consists in acceptance or rejection of the form of the *question*,

---

[1] F. G. French, *Common Errors in English* (London, 1949), p. 6. It should be noted that the point of view criticized here does not detract from the value of the practical exercises which the book contains.

and not, as in English, of the *facts*. It so happens that Japanese, and at least three Bantu languages, although in other respects very different from each other, *agree* in this point in *disagreeing* with English.[1] There can be no doubt that this error is due to interference from L1 and the same can be said of most such errors.

Comparison of L1 and L2 has been referred to as providing 'background material' in language teaching. This means that it should partly determine the selection and grading of items included in a course for students with a particular L1, and should influence the design of drills, exercises, and achievement tests. Moreover, a comparative knowledge of L1 and L2 is a useful part of the *teacher's* equipment, enabling him to predict and sometimes prevent errors, and to understand them more completely when they occur. As part of the technique of presentation—that is, as an actual classroom teaching device—explicit comparison of L1 with L2 may be valuable for certain types of pupil. Opinions on this, as on so many language-teaching matters, are divided. On the whole, the practice is not recommended in this country; in the Soviet Union, on the other hand, comparison of Russian with English (or other L2's) is regarded as a valuable part of the recommended process of teaching languages consciously. By means of comparison, the pupil is made more aware of the nature and working of his own and the second language, and this has considerable educational value.[2]

The study of language in linguistic terms is at least as important in relation to the description of L2. As Professor Quirk points out, a good deal of the traditional description of English is unsatisfactory, not so much because it is English in Latin terms as because it is English in non-linguistic terms.

[1] Cf. Samuel E. Martin, *Essential Japanese* (Tokyo, 1954), p. 364; Ethel O. Ashton, *Swahili Grammar* (London, 1944, edn of 1947), p. 79; T. Price, *Elements of Nyanja* (Nyasaland, 1947), p. 253. I am informed that the same is also true of Kikuyu.

[2] Cf., for example, V. D. Arakin, *Metodika Prepodavanija angliĭskogo jazyka* (Moscow, 1950), and *Metodika načal'nogo obučenija inostrannym jazykam*, ed. I. V. Karpov and I. V. Rakhmanov (Moscow, 1957).

An important characteristic of linguistics is something that I might call scientific optimism, a belief that language is describable. In the past hundred years, we have seen this attitude largely replace pre-scientific pessimism in one sphere of language teaching at least—namely, the teaching of pronunciation. Nowadays, we rarely hear statements that this or that sound 'cannot be described' or that one must be born west of the Severn in order to be able to pronounce Welsh *ll*, and the like. Phonetics, formerly an ancillary of academic comparative-historical linguistics, was brought into the market-place of language teaching through the efforts of nineteenth-century scholars like Jespersen, Storm, Viëtor, Passy, and Sweet. The student or teacher of English is particularly well supplied with good descriptions of pronunciation.

But the old pessimism still reigns to a large extent in the grammatical and lexical spheres. The student is still left to 'pick up' some features of English without the aid of specific instruction or drill. The so-called 'interjections' are a case in point. I know of no practical English grammar for foreign learners which describes the use of *oh*, *ah*, or the introductory or resumptive *well*. And yet the occurrences of these words, like the occurrences of all linguistic items, are not random: they are systematic and presumably describable. Compare, for instance, the use of *oh* and *ah* in the following piece of conversation, noting at the same time the accompanying differences of stress and intonation:

(*a*) Is that your hat? No. *Oh*, I thought it WAS.
(*b*) Is that your hat? Yes. *Ah*, I THOUGHT it was.

Or consider the following, which could be an extract from a story:

(*a*) Now, this man, his name was—*oh*, Johnson or something like that.
(*b*) Now, this man, his name was—*ah*, Johnson, that was it.
(*c*) Now, this man, his name was—*well*, Johnson, let's say. That's as good a name as any.

In these examples, *oh*, *ah*, and *well* are not interchangeable in a random way.

IV

It is not only in relation to categories of, perhaps, marginal utility—such as interjections—that one finds this kind of pre-scientific pessimism. The English prepositions, for example, are often presented as a category of baffling intractability whose usage cannot be described or explained. The English tenses are treated with almost equal despair.

I recently looked into five different books on English grammar for foreign learners and noted how they dealt with the eight 'basic' English verb forms: *talk, am talking, have talked, have been talking, talked, was talking, had talked, had been talking*. Each book listed 'the uses', or meanings, of these forms, but the number of uses ranged from 13 to 43! The actual figures were 13, 17, 21, 26, and 43. The foreigner may well despair of ever mastering the intricacies of English when he finds such disagreement among authorities. Is our language really so indeterminate? And, if so, why stop at forty-three uses? Since every occurrence is a different 'use' the number might well be infinite.

This is linguistic description without linguistics. In spite of wide divergences of view about most things, linguists are generally agreed on one point—that is, the systematic or, better, *systemic* nature of language. To some extent, almost all modern linguists are influenced by such views as the following, advanced by the great Swiss linguist Ferdinand de Saussure, that 'la langue est un système dont tous les termes sont solidaires et où la valeur de l'un ne résulte que de la présence simultanée des autres'.[1] Many of us would not agree that a language is describable as a single total system: but it is certainly possible and fruitful to describe parts of a language in terms of systems. The 'value' which terms derive from membership in a system is a *contrastive* value. What you say means what it means because it contrasts with the things you

[1] *Cours de linguistique générale* (Paris, 1949), p. 159.

might have said, but did not. To describe a system of tenses in linguistic terms, one must consider the values set up by the contrastive relationships between the items. Moreover, as Professor Quirk points out (p. 29), many kinds of signalling or communication about experience are reducible to binary contrasts—contrasts of the 'yes or no', 'on or off' type. A system of eight elements can be described in terms of three binary contrasts.[1]

It turns out that the eight basic English tense forms can be so described. First, each tense-unit contains either a *present* form (as the first member of complex units like *have been talking*) or a *past* form (*had been talking*); second, each form does or does not contain some part of the auxiliary *have* (*have talked~talk, had been talking~was talking*); third, each form does or does not contain some part of the auxiliary *be* (*am talking~talk, had been talking~had talked*).

In other words, these tense forms contrast in three possible ways; that is, they form a three-dimensional system of binary contrasts, as shown in the diagram overleaf.

The optimistic assumption of linguistics is that this set of three binary contrasts of form can be correlated with a corresponding set of meanings, and it remains to discover just what these contrastive, distinctive, meanings are. The traditional approach, not being systematically orientated, ignores the challenge. Moreover, it tends to assume that such traditional labels as 'present', 'past', 'continuous', are descriptions of meanings. As such, they are evidently inadequate. For example, we have 'presents' that refer to the future or the past, 'pasts' that refer to the present or future ('It's high time he *went*'), 'futures' that refer to the present ('He'*ll be* there now'), 'continuous' forms that refer to discontinuous activities, and so on. Observing that the apparently descriptive labels do not adequately describe, tradition has it in effect that 'the description doesn't fit the language: therefore, there is something wrong with the language'. English is said to be

[1] That is, any unit is (1) either in the first four or second four of the eight, (2) if it is in the first four it is either in the first two or the second two, (3) if it is in the first two it is either No. 1 or No. 2.

hopelessly illogical, and the description is patched up with a list of partial rules and exceptions. The linguistic approach has it that 'the description doesn't fit the language: therefore, there is

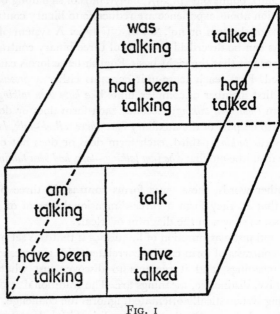

FIG. 1

something wrong with the description'. And this is a stimulus to making a more penetrating linguistic analysis.

V

The structural approach to language—the view that language is systemic, or describable in terms of systems of contrastive elements —has other implications of importance for our subject. The world at large is a continuum, an amorphous mass. Language is discrete. The language we speak forces us to select and group elements of our experience of the world in ways which it dictates. It provides a kind of grid, or series of grids, through which we 'see' the world, dissected along lines laid down by the systems of the language.

Language is systemic at all levels. Its phonological systems oblige us to produce, and to attend to, just those features of the total human sound-producing potential which are utilized distinctively, contrastively. The grammatical systems of English likewise oblige us to attend to certain distinctions and not to others: in the verbal system, for instance, the distinction between (*I*) *write* and (*I*) *am writing*. The verbal system of French forces no such distinction upon its speakers. Vocabulary, too, is systemic. The English system of terms for parts of the body obliges us, in ordinary everyday discourse, to make a rigorous distinction between *legs* and *feet*; but there is no such obligation upon speakers of many other languages—for example, Russian, Czech, Austrian-German, and Arabic. On the other hand, Russian obliges its speakers to distinguish between what may be called 'autokinetic' motion (*xodit'* meaning 'to go on foot, or by the goer's own effort'), and 'allokinetic' motion (*ezdit'* meaning 'to go on an animal or vehicle'); English can be indifferent to this distinction, with the neutral verb *go*.

It is such non-correspondences between the systems—and hence between the constituent elements of the systems—of English and other languages, which underlie many of the difficulties of learning English as a secondary language. The following more detailed illustration will make this clearer.

Fig. 2 is a diagram of a set or system of spatial relations; these relations vary, or contrast, in two dimensions. Strictly speaking, variations in the type of relation occur only in the horizontal dimension—in columns A, B, and C. The relation in column A is one of static *contiguity*, those in B and C are dynamic relations which may be termed *arrival* or *approach* (B) and *departure* or *separation* (C). The variations in the vertical dimension (in rows 1, 2, and 3) represent, on the other hand, different types of endpoint, or 'second term', for the relations represented. In row 1, we have relations concerned with the *exterior* of something. This contrasts with row 3, where the relations concern the *interior* of something. Between these, in row 2, we have relations which are indifferent with regard to the *exteriority* or *interiority* of the second. More simply, we may say that row 1 shows relations to a *surface* (or line), row 2 relations to a *point*, row 3 relations to a *space*.

Now, this is not just a 'logical' scheme of relations conjured

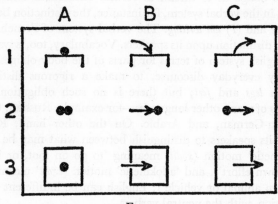

FIG. 2

out of nowhere. It is, on the contrary, a system which has been set up for the description of the meanings of a group of common English prepositions. This group of prepositions provides a 'grid' which can be placed over Fig. 2, and which 'fits' it exactly—necessarily so, of course, since the system of relations in Fig. 2 is derived from it.

If Fig. 2 had been a purely 'logical' scheme, we might, for instance, have completed it with a fourth column, D, showing *static separation*, parallel with the *static contiguity* of column A. It happens, however, that, though English obliges us, a good deal of the time, to make explicit (by selection of prepositions) the distinction symbolized by columns A versus B, there is rarely any such obligation to distinguish C from static separation.

It is hardly necessary to give examples of the more 'concrete' uses of these prepositions, but the systematic distinctions hold good also for expanded or less obvious uses. Compare, for example, (a) *on entering the room, he sat down*; (b) *in entering the room, he tripped over the mat*; (c) *at his entrance, everyone stood up.* In (a) his *sitting down* is subsequent, and thus *external*, to his entering:

	A	B	C
1	on	onto	off
2	at	to	(away) from
3	in	into	out of

FIG. 3

hence *on.* In (b) his *tripping* is part of the actual process of entering, and thus *internal* to it: hence *in.* In (c) his *entrance* merely marks a point in time; the question of the precise simultaneity or otherwise, or the 'exteriority' or 'interiority' of the *standing up* in relation to the entrance, is left open: hence *at.*

Another feature of the system, which is not brought out in Fig. 3, is that the prepositions in column A are more widely used than those in column B. Of the two sets, we may say that those in column B are 'marked' (compare the discussion of marked and unmarked members of pairs in Professor Quirk's paper, pp. 29 ff), and hence more restricted in application than those in column A. Consequently, we find a tendency to use the more neutral, unmarked, 'static' A forms whenever the idea of directed motion, implying *approach* or *arrival*, is already covered by the accompanying verb. Thus we often *put* things *on* or *in* (rather than *onto* or *into*): we *arrive at* or *in* or, rarely, *on* (not *to* or *into*), we *aim at, fire at,* and so on, and we can make distinctions like *throw to* and *throw at,*

155

and *talk to* (the normal, neutral, form) and *talk at* (implying pointed, directed, 'aggressive' talking), and so on.

The use of English prepositions gives foreign learners a good deal of trouble. But here, as elsewhere, some clarification results if we regard them not as isolated, independent items, but as units in a contrastive system deriving their values from the inter-relationships between them.

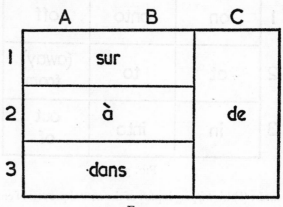

FIG. 4

This 'grid' shows that in the French language one can be indifferent (in so far as selection of prepositions is concerned) to the contrast between relations of *static contiguity* (A), and *approach* (B), though distinctions between the different types of end-term (1, 2, 3) are made here somewhat as in English. For the *separation* relation (C), French, on the other hand, is indifferent to the end-term discriminations (1, 2, 3) which are obligatory in English.

Fig. 4 shows how approximately the same semantic field as that indicated in Figs. 2 and 3 is 'dissected' by a roughly corresponding sub-system of prepositions in French.

Fig. 5 indicates how roughly the same field is covered by the system of 'local cases' in Finnish: 'adessive' (*-lla*), 'inessive' (*-ssa*), 'allative' (*-lle*), 'illative' (*-V-n*), 'ablative' (*-lta*), 'elative' (*-sta*).[1]

[1] In (-V-n), 'V' means (graphic) repetition (phonological lengthening) of the stem-final vowel, the commonest form of the illative suffix, as in *talo* 'house', *taloon*.

Finnish distinguishes rigorously between *exteriority* and *interiority*, but lacks the neutral, or indifferent, series (2) of English.

	A	B	C
1	-lla	-lle	-lta
2 3	-ssa	-V-n	-sta

FIG. 5

These somewhat crude and over-simplified examples will serve to illustrate the point I am making: namely, that systems of different languages impose different 'grids' on our experience of the world. These grids are rarely, if ever, isomorphic (that is, identical in form); consequently there is no correspondence between systems, or between their constituents, which derive their values from their interrelations within the systems.[1]

One of the more obvious implications of this kind of non-correspondence is that, in a certain sense, 'complete' translation is impossible. A sentence in one language may be appropriate to exactly the same practical situation as a sentence in another language. But in the linguistic sense, the two versions can never have exactly the same 'value', and this may have more than purely theoretical importance. The main defect of the so-called 'Grammar-Translation Method' was not that it used grammar translation, but that it used them badly. Ignoring the systemic

[1] The reader may draw his own conclusions about the practical results of the non-correspondences illustrated here. Some of them are well-known 'common errors' of French or Finnish speakers of English.

nature of language, it *equated* grammatical categories and lexical items of L1 and L2 in an atomistic way, as if they were directly equivalent, instead of being units deriving incommensurable values from the different systems of L1 and L2.

VI

Finally, the view of language as systemic is very relevant to the problem of 'thinking' in a language. It is sometimes said that the teacher of English as L2 must aim to get his pupils 'thinking in English'. A pupil is often said to 'think in English' when he appears to respond to situations automatically and immediately in English, without first verbalizing his experience in L1 and then translating. But it seems to me to be taking a somewhat superficial view to call this 'thinking in English'. Many will be familiar with the fluent, automatically responding dragoman, who can patter inaccurately in several languages. Conscious pre-verbalization in L1, and translation into L2, may be entirely suppressed, but errors due to interference from L1 still keep breaking through. In so far as that occurs, I should not say that the speaker is 'thinking in English', however fluently he may be making English-sounding noises.

For me, the phrase 'thinking in English' refers to something more fundamental: namely, applying the English 'grids' to experience—categorizing directly in the terms laid down by the systems of the English language. The Frenchman who says 'I have gone to the cinema yesterday', and the Russian who says 'My foot hurts' when he has injured his leg, may be responding automatically and immediately in English: but they are categorizing in terms of French and Russian systems respectively. That is to say, the linguistic values of the verb form *have gone*, in the one case, and the lexical item *foot*, in the other, are those set up by systems in French and Russian, even though their phonological shapes may be purely English.

The merit of 'Direct Method' teaching is supposed to be that it sets up immediate associations between situations and linguistic forms. In so far as it succeeds in this it may establish the kind of superficial automatism referred to above: but it will not *necessarily* lead to 'thinking in English' in the more fundamental sense. To achieve this end, we must try to teach our pupils to make the kinds of discriminatory response that a native English speaker makes. We must train them to respond selectively in English to those particular contrastive features of experience which are linguistically significant in English—to those contrastive values which are set up by the interrelation of terms within systems of the English language. To some extent, this need is intuitively grasped by all good teachers. But linguistic analysis makes the problem explicit, and suggests that practical techniques for achieving the desired end should be based on a penetrating structural, or systemic, description of English as L2, and on comparisons between systems in English and roughly corresponding ones in L1.[1]

There is still a great deal of research to be done in this field, but there is little doubt that the 'study of language in linguistic terms' can contribute much of value to the Teaching of English as a Foreign Language.

[1] Such correspondences are always approximate. Here, as in some other spheres of applied linguistics (for example, mechanical translation and linguistic geography), one is obliged, in order to do useful work, to make comparisons which may not be justifiable on strict theoretical grounds.

BIBLIOGRAPHICAL INDEX

Reference is made (with full bibliographical details) to the following books and articles on the pages indicated:

Abercrombie, D., 'Gesture', 16
    Problems and Principles, 139, 144
Abercrombie, L., 'Principles of Literary Criticism', 113
Adams, C., ed., The Worst English Poets, 56
Allen, W., ed., Writers on Writing, 59
Allen, W. S., On the Linguistic Study of Languages, 12
Arakin, V. D., Rakhmanov, I. V., Metodika Prepodavanija angliĭskogo jazyka, 148
Armstrong, L. E., Ward, I. C., A Handbook of English Intonation, 82
Arthos, J., The Language of Natural Description in Eighteenth-Century Poetry, 56
Association of Assistant Mistresses in Secondary Schools, Memorandum on the
    Teaching of English, 3
Ballard, P. B., Teaching the Mother Tongue, 3
Bateson, F. W., English Poetry: A Critical Introduction, 27
Bazell, C. E., Linguistic Form, 29
Bell, R. W., 'Form, Style and Expression', 37
Blamires, H., English in Education, 3, 11
Brooks, C., Warren, R. P., Fundamentals of Good Writing, 37, 43, 46, 48
Bühler, K., The Mental Development of the Child, 61
Carroll, J. B., The Study of Language, 14
Catford, J. C., 'Intelligibility' and 'The Background and Origins of Basic
    English', 143
Cestre, C., Dubois, M.-M., Grammaire complète de la langue anglaise, 15
Cherry, C., On Human Communication, 66
    '"Communication Theory"—and Human Behaviour', 107
Collingwood, R. G., The Principles of Art, 107
Crossland, R. A., 'Graphic Linguistics and its Terminology', 19
Davie, D., Articulate Energy, 24
Dessoulavy, C., The Word-book of the English Tongue, 41
Dunkel, H., Second-Language Learning, 140
Eastman, M., The Literary Mind: its Place in an Age of Science, 132
Eddington, A., The Philosophy of Physical Science, 127
Education, Board of, The Teaching of English in England, 2, 9
    Suggestions for the Consideration of Teachers in Public Elementary Schools, 90
Education, Ministry of, Pamphlet No. 26, Language, 10
English Association, Pamphlet No. 56, The Problem of Grammar, 9
Evans, B. I., Literature and Science, 123